Modern Poetry in Tr
Series Three, Numbe

Freed Speech

Edited by David and Helen Constantine

MODERN POETRY IN TRANSLATION

Modern Poetry in Translation
Series Three, No. 12
© Modern Poetry in Translation 2009 and contributors
ISBN 978-0-9559064-2-8

Printed and bound in Great Britain by Short Run Press, Exeter

Submissions should be sent in hard copy, with return postage, to David
and Helen Constantine, *Modern Poetry in Translation*, The Queen's College,
Oxford, OX1 4AW. Unless agreed in advance, submissions by email will
not be accepted. Only very exceptionally will we consider work that has
already been published elsewhere. Translators are themselves responsible
for obtaining any necessary permissions. Since we do sometimes authorize
further publication on one or two very reputable websites of work that has
appeared in *MPT*, the permissions should cover that possibility.

Founding Editors: Ted Hughes and Daniel Weissbort

Subscription Rates: (including postage)

	UK	Overseas
Single Issue	£9.95	£12.50 / US$ 21
One year subscription (2 issues, surface mail)	£19.90	£25.00 / US$ 42
Two year subscription (4 issues, surface mail)	£36.00	£46.00 / US$ 77

To subscribe please use the subscription form at the back of the magazine.
Discounts available.

To pay by credit card please visit www.mptmagazine.com

Modern Poetry in Translation is represented in the UK by
Central Books, 99 Wallis Road, London, E9 5LN

For orders: tel +44 (0) 845 458 9911 Fax +44 (0) 845 458 9912
or visit www.mptmagazine.com

Modern Poetry in Translation Limited. A Company Limited by Guarantee.
Registered in England and Wales, Number 5881603.
UK Registered Charity Number 1118223.

Contents

what they have done. Saying is release, not saying is a continuing captivity. And if the sufferer can say the things well, make a story or a poem of them, or transpose them expressively into clay, stone, bronze, paint or a song, then it may feel that the things so uttered have not only been escaped from but also that they have been mastered. Some poems in this issue seem to have that faith. At the same time, all therapists know that the moment of release into utterance is fraught with risk: like leading the monster out of the labyrinth and in broad daylight looking it in the face. Can you face it? Reticence. Was it good or bad that so many men coming home from so many wars would not talk about them? Even in poems there is that risk. By saying unbearable things very exactly, they may confront us with more than we can bear.

In Classical literature there is a strong sense of what should not be said or of what cannot be borne if it is said. When Oedipus by his own insistent questioning hauls his past out into the daylight it is unbearable. Jocasta hangs herself and he puts out his eyes. Then Creon says he must be shut up in the house: he is unfit to be looked at by the daylight. In his case freed speech is a catastrophe. He has things in him which are unspeakable and by his own insistence, by his helpless desiring to know the truth, they get spoken.

Oedipus the King is a play in verse. By its beauty of form it renders (just about) bearable what by the beautiful force of its language it reveals. One cardinal fault in some contemporary poetry is the saying of personal things unshaped and unformed, merely as they come, in a language too little removed from common speech. The effect of this is more often lamentable than unbearable. Such poetry follows (where it should resist) the contemporary willingness to say anything at any time anywhere. People bellow their private lives in the Quiet Coach into mobile phones; they confess on television, on the front pages of the daily newspapers and on the web. And in the choice of words there is nearly no sense now of any that should not be uttered whenever you please. Poetry, unless it resists, gets swept along on this tide of slovenly bad language. It is a freeing of speech into its own degradation. No writer or translator of poetry can be glad of that.

Heinrich Heine, living in Paris but publishing largely in German in Germany, was used to having his works censored by the Prussian authorities. Briefly in 1848, the year of revolutions, there was no censorship. He said, 'Alas, I can't write any more. I can't, for there's no censorship. How can a person who has always lived under censorship write without it? There'll be no style any more, no grammar, no decency. Till now when I wrote something stupid I thought, never mind, the censor will cross it out or change it. I relied on good censorship. But now I feel very unhappy and at a loss. I keep hoping it's not true and that the censor is still there.'

Heine was being ironic – but not totally. The censor, he felt, did wonders for his style. And for his cunning, for the whole art of effective reticence, clever allusiveness, saying-not-saying. Every writer needs a censor: not a policeman, not a priest, not a Home Secretary, but some cool, close, critical reader over your shoulder who won't let anything sloppy, self-indulgent, superfluous, inchoate, merely personal through. And that same friendly reader might have a sackful of shapes and forms to hand, rhyme-schemes and metres, tones, dialects and traditions, like a cabdriver's 'knowledge', to help you bind your freed speech and make it work.

David and Helen Constantine
August 2009

The Next Issue of MPT

The next issue of *Modern Poetry in Translation* (Third Series, Number 13, spring 2010) will be called 'Transplants'.

Translation can be thought of as the transplanting of a living thing out of its native time and place into somewhere foreign. There it may thrive or die. We invite submissions that will test and exemplify that idea. We should be especially glad to consider contributions that showed, and perhaps also discussed, how particular *forms* of poetry may be transplanted across time and space. Must they be modified? Or can the host culture be induced to accept them as they are? The Earl of Surrey translated *Aeneid* II and IV into iambic pentameters, judging that they would serve better than Virgil's hexameters. With examples from all three genres – epic, dramatic and lyric – we should like to assemble a variety of the ways and means by which a literary transplant's chances of survival may be increased.

Submissions should be sent by 1 February 2010, please, in hard copy, with return postage, to The Editors, Modern Poetry in Translation, The Queen's College, Oxford, OX1 4AW. Unless agreed in advance, submissions by email will not be accepted. Only very exceptionally will we consider work that has already been published elsewhere. Translators are themselves responsible for obtaining any necessary permissions. Since we do sometimes authorize further publication on one or two very reputable websites of work that has appeared in *MPT*, the permissions should cover that possibility.

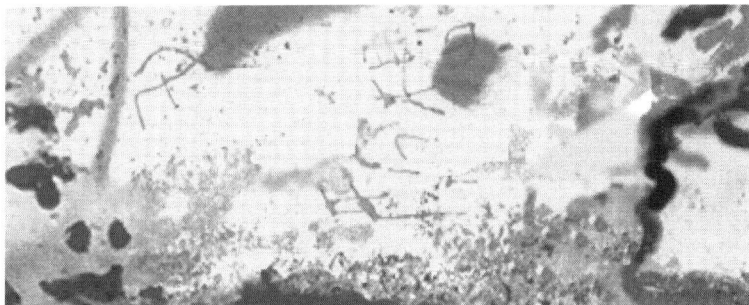

See How I Land: Oxford poets and exiled writers

In autumn 2008, the Oxford Brookes Poetry Centre, in partnership with the Oxford charity Asylum Welcome, launched a new initiative: the 'Oxford Poets and Refugees project'.

The project, funded by the Arts Council, brought together fourteen published Oxford-based poets and fourteen exiled writers, most of whom were refugees and asylum-seekers. Each established poet worked one-to-one with an exiled writer over a series of three half-day workshops, held at Oxford Brookes in November and December 2008, and led by Carole Angier.

One of our main objectives for the project was to facilitate the production of new, high-quality, thought-provoking literature. We also wanted to enhance readers' awareness of the human stories behind the politically-charged issue of immigration. But, perhaps most of all, we wanted to give a voice to those whose voices are seldom heard, and whose stories are so often deemed 'lacking in credibility' by the UK asylum system.

Each pair worked together on a piece of poetry or prose which was written by the refugee and mentored by the established writer. Each established writer also wrote a poem arising from or inspired by the experience. And, finally, each pair produced a jointly-authored prose statement providing a context for the two main pieces – explaining, for instance, where the ideas came from, whether or not translation was involved, and how particular words or forms were agreed upon.

The resulting work has been collected into an anthology, *See How I Land: Oxford poets and exiled writers* (Heaventree Press, 2009), and the contributions from two of the pairs who participated in the project – Dawood and Jamie McKendrick, and Yousif Qasmiyeh and Bernard O'Donoghue – are featured here.

Carole Angier, Rachel Buxton, Stephanie Kitchen, and Simon White

Dawood
Jamie McKendrick

We spent the three workshops talking about Dawood's journey from Iran to Britain. Dawood has learnt some English, but for the details of his story we needed the expert assistance of Sheherazade McKean, a Farsi interpreter.

There must now be many hundreds of thousands of parallel and similarly epic journeys undertaken by people desperate to leave impossible situations, each one in its own way both unique and representative. These journeys require courage and endurance, particularly for those – the majority – with little money, and often subject the travellers to unbearable hardships. Even if they reach their intended destination, a whole new set of difficulties and uncertainties awaits them. When Dawood set off from Iran to Turkey he was in a group of a hundred and fifty people, mainly from Afghanistan, Iran and Pakistan. Along the way he was prey to ruthless exploitation by various paid 'agents' who were responsible for arranging the stages of his journey, as well as utterly dependent for his survival on his fellow-travellers, and on the rare acts of goodwill he encountered. Many die en route, and most well know the risks they are running.

Dawood, who has written many poems before leaving Iran and

since arriving in Britain, has offered one of these, 'Night Letter',
for the anthology. This was fluently and effectively translated by
Sheherazade. It deals with the bitter experience of exile. The only
explanatory note which the translator suggested it might need
concerns the image of the rainbow-like tablecloth – this refers
to the colourful array and variety of the neighbour's food rather
than to the fabric of the cloth itself.

Jamie's poem relates to a small portion of Dawood's story. It
deals freely with the material, and though written in the first
person, makes no pretence to speak in Dawood's own voice.

Dawood and Jamie

Night Letter

sometimes I scribble over my name with a black pen
to leave no trace though maybe a trace remains
sometimes I see a dead sun in the looking glass
as I look at myself I paint the mirror black
I always write about the moon and sun
night scares me yet I write about the moon
tonight and every night I'll write a night letter
a stricken letter from the stars to the moon
saying how darkness suffers from the lack of moonlight
our sun was asleep – God's will had veiled it
if I say God does not exist I may be hanged
they'll call me an atheist – God will be angered
my God knows only that I'm homeless wandering
close by the sea longing for a drop of water
my next door neighbour's daughter sleeps hungry
when she asks for bread her mother says there's none
misery is all my brother's seen since youth

this was his destiny my mother said – God did not care
another neighbour plays with bread
God slips between the fingers of his hands
his tablecloth's more vivid than the rainbow
we are as different as the earth and sky
though both of us are human born into the same world
if this is how I had to be – maybe God's will was unwilling
why was He not willing? Did I not pray enough?

Dawood

Odyssey

'Burly, unscareable, only the rats
were at home in the camp at Patra
– you can see for yourself this foyer of hell
if you go on holiday to Greece.
I stayed, unsure how to leave, nine months in all,
apart from the two days in hospital
after being picked up by the police.
I survived, unlike Ali
whom I'd been with from the start – we'd argued
and agreed every step of the way, walking by
night through the mountains to Turkey,
avoiding landmines, praying for rain
to drink, rationing out the tinned food
we'd thought to bring, our trainers in tatters.

That day we had a lunch of rice
then said goodbye. He chose a lorry
he was hoping would board the ferry
to Ancona. You have to hold on for

dear life above the back axle
to a sheaf of oily wires – one pot-hole,
a sudden stop or an acceleration,
and chances are you'll lose your grip and fall.
To send his body back to Iran
would have cost many times more than
the few dollars we kept hidden
in a bar of soap, carefully hollowed out
and sculpted over. All we could do
was bury him by the camp at Patra.'

Jamie McKendrick

Yousif Qasmiyeh
Bernard O'Donoghue

From our first meeting in November 2008, Yousif expressed concerns that the term 'asylum-seeker/refugee' was featuring so prominently as an overarching heading for this poetry project. Being a refugee should not require foregrounding one's legal condition above all else, overshadowing, for instance, one's personal, professional and writing history beyond and before asylum.

Both members of this writing partnership are outsiders: Yousif is a Palestinian refugee by birth, having been born in a Lebanese-based Palestinian refugee camp; Bernard is Irish.

When Carole Angier proposed a 30-second, quick-response exercise to devise an image, Bernard, like most people in the room, invoked an idyllic, and perhaps rather defensive image of his home or family, set in his native area of North County Cork. For the larger initial writing project, he responded to Carole's suggestion of writing a letter to an earlier self by situating himself as a nine-year-old Bernard. This was a fun, and yet unremarkable creative process, perhaps the natural response of someone who has had a relatively free and unpoliticised life.

Yousif, on the other hand, responded to the first exercise with the idea of 'holes'. Initially, perhaps, this idea was provoked by the gap between the request for an instant image and the eventual response. However, the notion of 'holes' immediately widened to include a range of meanings and implications. In our subsequent meeting, this proved very productive, and Yousif planned to write a poem – closely following a modernist structure – constituted around a series of episodes: that is, holes with holes between them on the page.

The fundamental opposition which emerged is whether 'holes' are seen as destructive or creative; clearly, they can be both. We recalled the story of the Dutch boy who put his thumb in the hole of a dam and saved his country from the floods. Perhaps a further challenge is to explore an uncomfortable, intermediate position between the two. The pre-holed condition is also the child's link with the mother at birth, while the final 'hole' is arguably death. It is important, we agreed, to distinguish 'holes' from 'gaps': the latter are examples of discontinuity, with little sense of anything deeper.

Unlike gaps, 'holes' can be seen as ingredients of a larger entity. They may even be that which ultimately defines the entity. They are also considered to be active concealers of things, and one of Yousif's episodes explores this 'holey' function. Indeed, in keeping with the ambiguity of 'holey/holy' roles, Yousif's father rejected his son's temporary infatuation with the notion of prophecy, favouring his son's incorporation into the more productive activities of shop-keeping. It is interesting to ponder the possible trajectories of these two callings, and to ask whether the child's first preference is still acted on in the adult's writings. We quoted Dryden's 'great wits are sure to madness near allied': prophecy, like madness, can be seen as a hole in the mind, with the corresponding possibilities of destruction and creation.

In addition, we discussed the issues which arise with the term 'hole' itself in English, especially its – productive or complicating

– homophone 'whole'. This was exploited by Yeats in his risqué poem 'Crazy Jane talks with the Bishop': 'For nothing can be sole or whole/ That has not been rent.'

Concluding our reflection is the recognition that translation is complex, yet artificial: this is its difficulty but also its possibility. The first issue, of course, is the problem faced by a Palestinian poet working towards publishing in English. Writing poetry in a language other than the mother tongue is immeasurably difficult (yet often with intriguing outcomes), and Yousif continues to prefer writing in Arabic and translating his own work into English.

Yousif and Bernard

Holes

1

How will I die
While all
Can see me?

2

When is the rain
Going to admit
Its fall?

3

I was born
On the seam of a dress,
In the last hour
Of the sixth day,
Between clusters of stars
And the borders of a river.

I was neither
Adam reaching the ground,
Nor was I myself
In cities
Which share their water
With the agents of doom.

4

I lean on
The footsteps of my past
As I slip towards
My shadow.

The shadow which I left
Lying
Outside our house
On the morning
Of that funeral.

I am that dead person
But I don't know
How
He managed to escape.

5

May we watch the rain falling,
And may we follow its rhythm
Like those bereaved of children.

May we count the moons
That evening:
A moon for every face,

And for every exile,
As they roll their prayer beads
Along the journey.

6

They said: Here is the *accoucheuse*
Who dropped you
Off her hunch
And screamed,
On behalf of your mother,
At the crowded heads
To disperse
A shade
So the air
Might reach you;

So your trembling mother
Might place you
At the threshold
Of the shrine
Before the holy man's tomb,
With three
Thick candles
That the widow
Of the guardian
Would light
Once you awoke.

7

I can almost
Hear
Her exhalation
In that wind-shaken coffin,
On the shoulders
Of those
Who hoped
To hunt the moon down
With their prayers.

8

The flock of frightened angels
I follow,
Roaming at a low height
In the morning of the war.
I say:
Please stop,
So you can return safely
To your dead ones.

9

Slowly,
The caravan descends
With no invocation on the window
To save its passengers
From envy.

Those on board
Spend their time
Collecting cocoons
In ashen bags.

A black woman
Who has tapped
With her shoes
The courier's head
Alights, and enters the tunnel.
She kisses the charm on her chest
And punctures her neck.

10

Upside down
And in the middle
Of the yard
His picture was hung.
They did not change
The place of the pail.
He will cry,
And the image
Will float on the
Face of the pail.

Yousif Qasmiyeh

Emigration
for Yousif Qasmiyeh

Unhappy the man who keeps to the home place
and never finds time to escape to the city
where he can listen to the rain on the ceiling,
secure in the knowledge that it's causing no damage
to roof-thatch or haystack or anything of his.

Unhappy the man who never got up
on a tragic May morning, to go to the station
dressed out for America where he might have stood
by the Statue of Liberty, or drunk in the light
that floods all the streets that converge on Times Square.

Unhappy the man who has lacked the occasion
to return to the village on a sun-struck May morning,
to shake the hands of the neighbours he'd left
a lifetime ago and tell the world's wonders,
before settling down by his hearth once again.

Bernard O'Donoghue

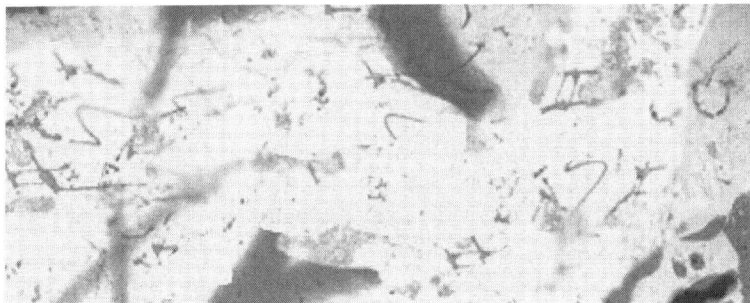

Editorial

So far as poetry is concerned, speech is freed – given utterance – in the writing of the poem. There's a paradox in that. Speech is freed by being enclosed in the form of a poem. In German 'gebundene Rede' ('bound speech') is verse. True, there's 'free verse'; but 'free', when such verse works, actually means abiding by rules, often very strict rules, of the poem's own devising.

The language of a poem is not 'freed' by being translated; it is moved into the rules and forms of another language. But in that process the effect of the poem is *enlarged*: and not just in that word's modern sense – increased, extended – but in the archaic sense too, set free, given its liberty. The translated poem has a new land to run free in.

The very first issue of *MPT* was an act of extending and releasing. Publishing Herbert, Holub, Miłosz, Popa and Voznesensky in English, Hughes and Weissbort enlarged them into a wider territory. Several contributors to this issue – *MPT*, Third Series, Number 12 – nearly half a century later, do the same. There are poems in these pages which have never been translated into English before; and some translations that bring us news from places we are lucky not to have known.

Much therapy rests on the belief that saying is better than not saying; that it helps to utter one's suffering. We talk of repression and release. People may be helped if they can say what has happened to them, what has been done to them or

Yannis Ritsos
'Tombs Of Our Ancestors'
Translated by Sarah Kafatou

We should protect our dead, their power, so that our enemies
don't dig them up some day and carry them off.
Without them we'd be in double danger. How could we live
without our houses, furniture, fields? Without, especially,
the tombs of our ancestors: warriors, wise men?
Remember how the Spartans stole Orestes' bones from Tegea.
Our enemies must never know where we buried them.
But how can we even know who our enemies are?
When will they come, where will they be coming from?
So, no impressive monuments, no elaborate decoration.
That would attract attention, envy. Our dead don't need it.
Frugal, chaste, silent now,
they don't care about honey, incense, empty rituals.
Better a plain stone, a pot of geraniums, a secret sign,
or nothing. For safety, keep them in our hearts, if we can.
Better if even we don't know where they're buried.
The way things are going now – who knows? –
we might dig them up ourselves, one day, and throw them
    away.

*(Ritsos, born a hundred years ago, was arrested following the Greek
military coup of 1967 and exiled to the island of Leros, where he wrote
this poem in 1968.)*

Yannis Ritsos
Four poems
Translated by Robert Hull

Rebirth

For years no one had taken care of the garden. Nevertheless,
this year – in May, in June – it was in bloom, of itself this
    time,
in one continuous blaze to the railings, a thousand
roses, carnations, geraniums, sweet peas –
violet, orange, green, red, yellow –
colours, plumes of colour – so much so that the woman
with her old watering-can appeared again to do the watering –
beautiful as before, calm, with a lovely indefinable assurance.
    And the garden
gathered round her, shoulder-high, it embraced her, took her
    completely;
it lifted her in its arms. Then we saw, in broad daylight,
how the whole garden, and the woman with her watering
    can, ascended – and as
we gazed skywards, some drops from her watering-can
fell gently on our cheeks, chin, lips.

Return

The statues left first. The trees soon after,
the people and the animals. The place
was utterly deserted. A wind came. Newspapers
hurried along the streets, and thorn-twigs.
At night the lights came on of their own accord.
On his own, a man came back; he looked round,
took out a key, and pressed it to the earth
as if passing it to an underground hand
or planting a tree. Afterwards he climbed
the marble steps and looked out over the city.
One by one, cautiously, the statues returned.

Fre – e - dom

You'll keep saying it
the same
plain word
the one
you lived for
and died for
were born again for
(how often ?)
that same word –

all night
like this
every night
under rocks
syllable after syllable
like a tap dripping
in the sleep of the man
athirst
drip after drip
over and over
under stones
night after night

counted off on the fingers
simply
the way you say
I'm hungry
the way you say
I love you

as simply as
at the open window
breathing

e - lef- the - ri - a .

A small invitation

Come, to the shining beaches – he murmured to himself –
here where the colours are festive, look,
in a place unpolluted by royals,
with their closed-in carriages, their official emissaries.

Hurry, I mustn't be seen – he whispered –
I'm an escapee from night
a thief from the dark.

My pockets are stuffed with sun,
and my shirt –

come, it's burning my chest and hands –
take it.

And there's something I have to tell you
that not even I should hear.

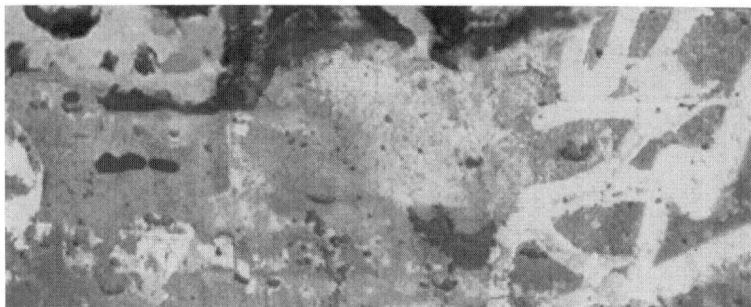

Berkan Karpat and Zafer Şenocak
'nâzım hikmet: on the ship to mars'
Translated by Tom Cheesman

In January 2009, the Turkish government announced that Nâzım
Hikmet (1901–1963) was to be rehabilitated. Deputy Prime
Minister Çiçek said, not quite apologetically: 'The crimes which
forced the government to strip him of his citizenship at that time
[in 1951] are no longer considered a crime.'

Formed by the Russian avant-garde as a student in Moscow
in the 1920s, Hikmet proclaimed the artist 'the engineer of the
human soul'. Many of his poems were set to music and some have
the status of folklore: they are so well known, people don't know
who wrote them. A major dramatist and novelist as well as poet,
and the author of a verse epic which some consider the greatest
Turkish-language work of his century, Hikmet was persecuted in
Turkey as a communist and spent most of his adult life in prison
or in exile. His prolific work makes his idealism poetically,
and above all accessibly, intelligible. Sufi poetry, with its rich
vernacular tradition, was an early and enduring influence, fused
with utopian modernism.

'nâzım hikmet: auf dem schiff zum mars' first appeared as a
pamphlet in 1998. This translation is based on the revised text in
Berkan Karpat and Zafer Şenocak's *futuristen-epilog. poeme* (2008).
That book collects five of their 'scenic poems'. The other four

speak of the defeated futurisms of revolutionary Russia, Turkish republican Kemalism, Robinson Crusoe, and Woyzeck and Marie. Each text was originally the lyrical component of a multi-media installation and theatrical production devised by Karpat, using layers of recorded sound and voices. In a series of such productions ('genesis-projects') since 1996, Karpat explores the modern history of 'inner utopias', the detritus of the themes of 'new man' and 'new world', in counterpoint with Anatolian mystic traditions. Şenocak is joint script-writer on most of these projects. Like Karpat, he is from Munich, with a Turkish background, only Şenocak now lives in Berlin. Writing in both German and Turkish, in his poetry Şenocak melds modernist perspectives with the preoccupations and forms of the medieval mystics. He has translated into German the work of Sufi poet Yunus Emre (c.1240–1320) and several contemporary Turkish poets. He is a fine essayist and novelist (in both languages) as well. In English are: *Door Languages* (poems translated from German by Elizabeth Oehlkers Wright, 2008) and *Atlas of a Tropical Germany: Essays on Politics and Culture, 1990–1998* (edited and translated from German by Leslie A. Adelson, 2000).

Şenocak relates how, during the putsch in Turkey in 1981, he narrowly escaped arrest for owning books by Nâzım Hikmet. He told the policeman that he was about to leave the country, and the books were not confiscated. Reading them with renewed interest for the first time since his teenage infatuation with Hikmet, he concluded that the political poems are 'dreadfully bad', because ideological partisanship is 'poison' for poetry. What remains are moving lyric poems of exile, loneliness, longing, travelling, in which Hikmet convincingly, memorably voices embodied life. Years later, Şenocak found in Karpat a collaborator who shared his dislike of the left's shibboleth saint Hikmet, as of the right's vilified traitor Hikmet (and, indeed, of the unread Hikmet, nowadays a nationalist hero purely because of his international fame), and his pleasure in the unaligned poet Hikmet. This is a writer whose language 'turns suffering and grief into energy', and still inspires, even if his sentimentality can invite pastiche. His

politics, though, can hardly be overlooked. Released from Turkish
jail, Hikmet became, in Şenocak's words, a 'hostage' in Stalin's
Russia, for all his freedom to travel and his other privileges: a
hostage of 'one of the twentieth century's ideological delusions,
which meant for millions of people exactly what Hikmet resisted
through his poetry all his life: unfreedom.' Karpat and Şenocak's
'dancing poem' is both homage and playful parody, a critical
tribute which dramatizes contradictions.

The translation takes a minimum of liberties. Many allusions
to texts by Hikmet, Rumi, and others probably escape me. For
those who may recognize them, I translate pretty literally. I
haven't tried to echo any of the existing English versions. One
allusion is in the proper name 'Kerem' (segment 2). A famous
poem, 'like kerem', expresses Hikmet's defiance, upon being
condemned to 28 years in prison in 1938. As translated by Larry
Clarke: 'i tell them: / let me be ashes / burning / burning / like
kerem / for if I do not burn / and if you do not burn / and if we
do not burn / who else / is here / to dis- / pel / the dark- / ness'.

The writers had to help me with *Schiffsrohr*, literally 'ship-
pipe' (segment 7). Karpat explained that they had engine-room
ironwork in mind, but it's also a pun on *Schilfsrohr*, reed flute,
and an allusion to Rumi's 'Ney nameh' ('The song of the flute'):
'Hear the reed complain. . . .'. 'Piping' is the nearest pun, but I'm
not sure it sounds right, which is always crucial. For instance, the
same section has 'announce' and 'lament' instead of 'proclaim'
and 'complain', to avoid rhyming with 'remain'.

Nâzım is pronounced with stress on the long a, z as in English,
and the second vowel unvoiced, so the syllable '-zım' sounds
rather like the end of 'communism'. Shemseddin of Tabriz is the
Sufi mystic a.k.a. Shams Tabrizi (d. 1248), the mentor, devotee
and 'intimate friend' (or lover) of Rumi (a.k.a. Mevlana, Maulana,
Molana) (1207–1273).

Leslie A. Adelson's essay 'Experiment Mars' (in *Über
Gegenwartsliteratur / About Contemporary Literature*, 2008) quotes
an earlier version of the translation, and gently criticizes it. My
thanks go to her for prompting me to try to do better.

nâzım hikmet: on the ship to mars

segment 1

tonight i am drinking sun
tonight on this ship
the sun from the veins of the machine
the literary machine
the machine room
from the machine room of the torturers
of the literary machine nâzım
i am drinking the voice of the sun
the sun from the veins of the tape reels
i am drinking shemseddin
two by two metres of darkspace
spin in my veins
in the veins of the tape reels
the machine nâzım
dreams

segment 2

in breaths between respites
i give birth to your voice
your frozen in iron crystals
voice
circles in its stalin corset
i spin in my round dance
between the scents of roses and machines
i stand
a flaming head
stand between
body slitters and slit bodies
crawl away

into the cell of my words
on this ship
i destroy
destroyer i
with my lyrical breath:
brother you are no tree in the forest

locked inside two by two metres
i crawl away into my singing
the singing
that shuts out my being mad
the singing thunders
knee deep in shit
i stand
and
roar my singing
my singing
against the walls of the ship's cell
against the walls i roar:
like kerem you shall burn
to burn like kerem
to ash i want
to burn roaring with my voice
i nâzım want to burn
to let there be light

i burn
with
green earth
red flag
white dove

i nâzım eat light

segment 3

and
so long as my heart still hangs from its branch
its dry strong blazing branch
i want to burn
i want to burn with nâzım in this darkspace
in my ship's cell
on my lips
the oil of the machines
i spin
in the oiled veins
of the machine
with the song of the sundrinkers
on my lips
to drink the sun from earthen bowls
drunkenly spin
with millions of red hearts
climb up my shiptower
climb higher and higher
i want
wanting
so long as my heart still hangs from its branch
in my chest
in my cell
of a chest
the dust from the archive spins
the tape reels of state security

comrade shemseddin

i spin
about myself
spin
about the nucleus
spin myself
i split
the nucleus
i engineer of souls
separated from the man i love
i drink from the black cup
from the sea of iron sperm
i give birth to the voice of nâzım
feet in salt
i stand
stand in the darkspace
longing for you
i drink
from the black cup

tonight
i split
nâzım
into
nâzım
each sound peeled away from my skin
nails memories into my skull

segment 4

in my skull night

at night in the starless
heavy sea
my face floats from me
beyond the memories
flows with the grains of light
in the water of the bosphorus
my skull dissolves
my skull in the pitchblack sewer
a butterfly
a butterfly
flown astray
into the room of somebody's life
shall i leave what my dust writes
on the ship's rough windows
as the name of the prisoner
shall i burn what my dust writes
with my red-hot sting
into your body
shall i drown in the sewer
with the red on my lips
drown in the shit

i roar light
on my lips
light
between my thighs
the white of the torturer
pulsates
in my crack
red
in the crack
red
the iron glows
in my guts
in my splayed wide
slit open
carnation flesh
the white laugh of my torturers
on my lips
light
as a folksong
on my lips
a song:
i nâzım want at last
our song

on my eyelid
the light glows
on my forehead the electric blue
the blue of the shredded butterfly
splays my guts
mills my veins
like a corpse on my chest
the light sleeps
i shut the madness in a song
shut my guts
below me the black stew
the black stew
rocks the ship
the black stew of the torturers
rocks me

segment 5

at night
when my jailbird slut
homeland
sleeps like a corpse on my chest
i dream:
nâzım
loves his country
and my nâzım must
love
his death-wish butterfly
country

and
he must
love
the black
brave look
the anatolian look
that is as open
and
true
     as a folksong
              on the lips
                      of the jailbird slut
              as the oath of the communists
hope is never defeated
never

and my nâzım must recite:
vladimir ilyich
                    when i say lenin
                    peace comes over me
                    trust in myself
                    trust in humankind and earth

my nâzım
must love his imprisonment
his two by two metres of darkspace
as one breaks bread
and dips it in salt
as the soft dusk falls
on the fishermen of istanbul
on the fishing workers
on on
peace comes over me
how peace comes over me
trust in myself
i
am an engineer
am a sound engineer
of sound good sense
i splice
in the blue
i splice
the fishermen to the sun

i nâzım am exhausted by my own burden
worn out by the weight of my hands
of my eyes and my shadows
my words pillars of fire
deep wells my words
a day will come
entirely unhoped-for
and
i cease to sing the song:
the world will be a single
giant cradle
for black
white
and yellow children
for all children of the world
a marvellous cradle
bedecked with light blue silken blankets

segment 6

i nâzım
am a simple turkish poet
tonight i am drinking sun
tonight on this ship
i nâzım
am a simple turkish poet
who is proud
to have dedicated
his brain
his heart
his pencil
and his whole life to his people
dedicated to the literary machine
the literary machine nâzım

prisoner in the machine room of the torturers
i am drinking the voice of the sun
the sun from the veins of the tape reels
i am drinking
brother shemseddin
i too had something to say about love
brother

when i was a child
i wanted to be a postman
a postman on a ship
but not on the rounds of a poet
just simply
a flesh and blood
postman
with my coloured crayons i drew postmen
hundreds and thousands of postmen
sent them through jules vernes novels
and through my atlases
nâzım the postman
that's me

segment 7

i want sleep at last
i nâzım on the way to the red planet
to drink the red
to sleep the red sleep
i did not find on the earth
red mars
hear the ship's piping
what it announces
now in the grey of my hair
only a shadow remains
in my heart a crack
hear how the piping laments
set alight by longing
the piping that burns in me
the piping of the torturers
twisted into the machine nâzım

i spin
spin myself
about myself
trrrrum
trrrrum
tiki
tak
trrrrum
trrrrum
trrrrum!
trak
tiki
tak!

segment 8

the feverish vocal cords
reel my words
into the grave
of shemseddin
into the machine room
where the sun is burned
shemseddin
you sun of tabriz
you i am drinking
i thirsting machine nâzım
i drink the stalin-nâzım
i drink the shemseddin-nâzım
i drink the poets' quarrel
i drink quarrel
i quarrel

lousily the veins of sound vibrate
my mood
i mood myself accordingly
presume a voice
your voice shemseddin
untune it
i am a worker
worker on the machine nâzım
tonight i am drinking shemseddin
tonight on this ship
the burned sun
from the veins of the machine
the literary machine
the machine room
from the machine room nâzım hikmet
i am drinking the voice of the sun

segment 9

for playing with
the red apple between the stars
for playing with between the stars
a giant red apple
a warm loaf
for one day at least
for a ship full of children
in salt
children turned into salt
as one breaks sun
and dips it in salt
between the stars
a ship full of children
in salt
children turned into salt
on the ship to mars

segment 10

as the tape heads grind round
can be made out:
most of nâzım was lost
only little remained ...

what do i care
as the digital heads grind round
can be made out:
most of me is lost
only little remains ...

what do i care
as the sounds are milled down
can be made out:
most was lost
only little remained . . .

what do i care

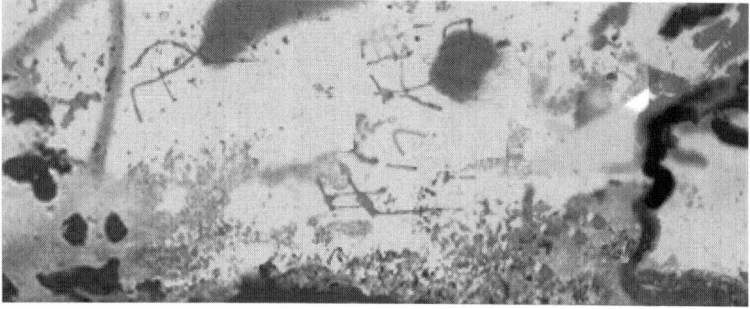

Edith Södergran
Four poems
Translated by Mike Horwood

Edith Södergran was born in St. Petersburg to Finland-Swedish parents in 1892. The family moved to the Finnish village of Raivola, in what was then a part of the Russian Empire and nowadays is part of Russia, when Edith was only a few months old. Later she attended the German High School of St. Petersburg, returning home to Raivola during the school holidays. Her education, obviously, was in German, and her earliest poems are almost all written in that language. Her mature work is written in Swedish.

Södergran's father died of tuberculosis in 1907 and Edith contracted the disease herself in 1908. She spent much of the following five years in sanatoria in Finland and Switzerland. The struggle against disease and the strength to overcome its debilitating effects are a recurring theme in her work. Another important influence was the intense and mystical relationship she had with nature and the entire universe.

Edith and her mother continued to live in Raivola through the years of the Russian Revolution which reduced them to poverty and near starvation. At times the fighting came within earshot and Raivola became virtually cut off from the outside world.

Södergran's first collection was published in 1916 and was

not generally well received, although she did have her defenders amongst the literary community of Helsinki. However, there were also hostile reviews and it is true to say that her work did not conform to contemporary styles and expectations and was not recognized or understood during her lifetime.

She had very little personal contact with literary circles, and that little gained her a reputation as an eccentric. Some described her as mentally unbalanced. After a brief stay in Helsinki, she returned to Raivola and never left again. She continued to write in virtual isolation until her death in 1923 at the age of thirty-one.

The poems published here are fairly free versions based on Södergran's originals, rather than strict translations.

Nordic Spring

My castles in the air have all melted like snow,
my dreams have run away like water.
Of all that I loved, only a blue sky
and a few pale stars remain.
The wind stirs itself between the trees.
Emptiness at rest. Silver-grey lake.
The old fir tree is awake and thinks
of a white cloud he kissed in a dream.

My Childhood Trees

The trees of my childhood rise high over the grass.
They shake their heads and ask: What have you done?
Each trunk is a reproach: You walk among us in disgrace.
You are a child, you can do anything,
why do you let your illness chain you?
You have become this objectionable character
we no longer recognise.
When you were childlike, you understood us,
your eyes were wise,
but now we'll tell you what the secret of your life is:
You will find the key to that secret in the grass on Raspberry
    Hill.
You need a jolt, you dreamer.
We'll soon wake you up from your sleep.

Instinct

My body is a mystery.
So long as my fragile figure breathes
you will know its power.
I will make the world free.
That's why the blood of Eros rushes to my lips
and his gold animates my limp hair.
By a mere glance,
sad or disillusioned, the world is mine.
Even as I lie suffering on my bed
I know: my feeble hand holds the world's fate.
Power flows in my unsteady step.
Power swings in the folds of my dress.
Power that you cannot resist.

The Land That Is Not

It is weariness of things as they are
that makes us long for the world that is not.
It is the land that the moon
speaks temptingly of.
It is the land where dreams come true,
our chains drop off
and the moon bathes our fevered brows.
Life has practised its deceptions
but I have come through at last –
to the land that is not.

In the land that is not
my lover walks, wearing the crown
I gave. On a moonless night
the stars should shine more brightly.
So whom do I love? Speak the name.
The black sky looks more distant than usual.
The earth is wrapped in fog
and we understand nothing,
but a child of the earth has its own certainty.
The child reaches its arms to the sky
for the answer: I love the one I will always love.

Ernst Stadler
Two poems
Translated by John Greening

These versions of German-speaking poets associated with the First
World War emerged as the surprising final push of a sequence of
verse letters I had been writing to the British war poets. We had
taken some sixth-form students to the battlefields and visited on
the last day the German cemetery at Langemark. Approaching
this bleakest of plots, the visitor sees four silhouetted figures in
battledress beyond the graves. It's a commemorative sculpture,
but it was in the back of my mind as I found myself turning from
Edward Thomas, Wilfred Owen, Edmund Blunden, Siegfried
Sassoon to poems by August Stramm, (1874–1915), Georg Trakl
(1887–1914), Georg Heym (1887–1912) and Ernst Stadler (1883–
1914). Heym, of course, did not live to see the war, but foresaw
it in his much-translated 'War' (1911). Stadler is less well known
outside Germany. He came from Alsace. He was a Rhodes Scholar
at Magdalen College, Oxford and is commemorated – as Poet
Scholar Soldier - in the cloisters there. He was killed near Ypres.

Pleasure in Form

First, bolts had to be broken, moulds
Be cracked before I let the world
Come bursting through new pipes: with form
Comes happiness and peace and warm
Contentment, yet I always need
To unplough what's been laid to seed.
Form wants to stifle and confine,
But I must sail beyond the line.
Form is pitiless, hard and clear,
Yet drives me to a stagnant mere.
Without the lifeline's dull insistence,
Life can sweep me out any distance.

Summer

My heart's standing up to its neck in yellow reaping light:
land that is ready to be harvested while the heavens smile.
A scythe-rattling singing will be heard through the fields
    soon.

My blood, in its marinade of happiness, attends,
absorbed completely by the noon heat.

The barns, the silos of my existence, bare for so long,
will let their entrances swing wide as lock-gates
and over the floors a golden vintage, an inundation, flow.

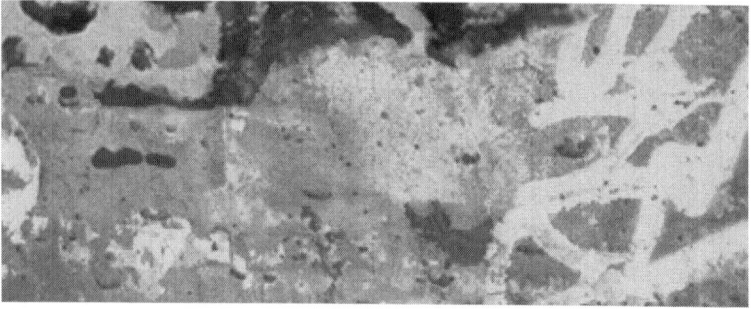

Gandhari's 'Lament' from the *Mahabharata*
Translated by Carole Satyamurti

The *Mahabharata* is one of the two great epic poems of India, composed around 2000 years ago. It is eight times as long as the *Iliad* and the *Odyssey* put together, and is a vast compendium of stories, teachings and much besides. But the narrative thread along which it is organised is the story of the lethal conflict between two sets of royal cousins, the Kauravas and the Pandavas, who compete for rule of the Bharata kingdom.

The conflict culminates in a terrible war, involving millions of men, on the plain of Kurukshetra. The war arises from the intransigence of the eldest Kaurava prince, Duryodhana and, after eighteen days of war, he lies dead, as do his ninety-nine brothers. The five Pandavas, guided by Krishna, an *avatar* of the god Vishnu, survive the bloodshed, and are victorious. But it is a pyrrhic victory, since so many of their allies, and all their sons, have been killed.

In this passage, the war is over, and Gandhari, queen, and mother of the Kauravas, surveys the battleground, strewn with the bodies of the dead. She has been given the temporary gift of divine sight, and can see and hear everything on the field. As in other epics, women are given relatively little voice in the *Mahabharata*, but here Gandhari seems to speak for any woman who has to stand by while men kill each other, and mourn them

afterwards. She, and nearly all the dead, belong to the order of
kshatriyas, the warrior caste.

Gandhari's Lament

I am Gandhari. Who am I now?
Childless mother of a hundred sons.
There should be a word for women such as I,
a word like 'widow', another word for 'empty'.

Ah! I can see the sweeping, blood-drenched plain
of Kurukshetra, in all its dreadful detail.

Everywhere is chaos, mangled flesh,
the aftermath of massacre. Everywhere
I look, in all directions, countless bodies
lolling in abandon, heads and limbs
at sickening angles, mouths gaping as if
their final cry should still be audible.
Eyes that shone with every heart-felt passion
now are empty pits, cleaned out by crows.
Gashes and holes in the silk of skin
show where a cunning spear has found its way
between the links of their bright, well-wrought mail.
Some wear their armour still, and seem unscathed
as if lapped in the luxury of sleep,
while others are half-naked, stripped of all
that marked them out from the mud they're made of.

Look at these fine young men, embracing Earth
as if discovered in the act of union
with a beloved bride – arms spread, their faces
oblivious to everything but this.
Oh, Earth has stolen them, Earth has triumphed
over all of us, defeated women.

What priceless wealth is scattered all around –
crowns, jewelled bracelets, ropes of gold
twisted round the muscled upper arms
of so many great warriors; anklets, torques,
all the regalia of rank. How useless
is that wealth – why, it could not protect them
from the smallest dart; and it doesn't keep
monsters and other scavengers from feasting
on their fat and flesh. Look at those storks,
tall as men, looking so disdainful
picking their way among the piled up corpses
yet ripping flesh from bone with cruel beaks
as ruthlessly as any rakshasa[1].

A month ago, who could have imagined
that men who loved the music of the bards
would now hear only the despairing cries
of their beloved wives. They who slept soft
now lie un-cushioned on the filthy ground.
Men who plunged in the sumptuous flesh of women
now sprawl, insensate, celibate for ever,
their rigid arms locked hard around a mace.

---

[1] Rakshasa – flesh-eating monster

Oh these poor women! Some are mute with shock;
most are wailing, shivering in their pain.
They call like cranes for mates who will never come.
Some try to find the body that belongs
with the head they love, then realise
it is not his. Some fail to recognise
the face of their own brother – beloved features
so destroyed by ravenous scavengers.

Here is Duryodhana! Ah! my tragic son,
caked in blood, your strong legs smashed, distorted,
your breast-plate still in place. I remember
how you looked when you asked for my blessing,
full of pride and foolish hope. I knew then
it must end in defeat. All I could manage
were luke-warm words – not what you most wanted,
not the heart-felt prayer for victory
men need from women when they go to war.

Time turns. You died a hero, Duryodhana.
Devoted women once fanned you to sleep;
now, only the wings of hungry birds
make a breeze about you. Here's your poor wife,
Lakshmana's mother, weeping for her son,
as well as for you. That broad-hipped, sexy girl
is huddling in the crook of your strong arm.
No more good times for her.

                            So many women,
washing blood off their men's dead faces,
whirling, lurching, screeching at the vultures
like lunatics. Women of all ages.
What must we have done in a past life?
What sin could have deserved this utter horror?

And, oh, my other fine sons! Here they lie;
distinct in life, with differing looks and gifts,
each with his individual voice, his laugh,
now carrion for indiscriminate crows.

Look! There is Abhimanyu, still beautiful,
that brilliant warrior who outshone even
his father. And there is Uttaraa, his wife,
pregnant with his child. She lies beside him
caressing him, kissing his cold face,
and now she has unbuckled his gilded mail
and stares intently at his many wounds:

'O Abhimanyu, my beloved husband,
my world, soul of my soul, how your injuries
gape for all to see. My heart, too, is pierced
by death's pitiless darts, but invisibly.
You were like Krishna in your strength and courage,
so alive. Yet now you sleep too soundly.
Oh, your skin is delicate as a girl's;
isn't the rough ground grazing you? You lie,
arms flung wide as though you are exhausted
by grinding labour. Rest, my love.'

                                                        She cradles
his head in her lap and strokes his tangled hair.

'Where were their hearts, those Kauravas who trapped
    you,
a solitary boy? Where were your uncles,
your natural protectors? How can a kingdom,
however rich, however well deserved,
be worth your life, my prince, my precious one?

Oh, I long to die! I want to join you!
But no one can die before the gods decide.
You lie here, lifeless; I have my wretched life.
In that world you've gone to, will there be
a woman to caress and laugh with you
as if she were me? O my Abhimanyu,
be happy in that afterlife, but remember
what I was to you, how we loved together!'

So many shields strewn on the bloody field
like fallen moons, and scattered spears and bows
shining like shafts of sunlight in the gloom. . . .

O, so much sorrow! It is women's fate
to love and lose, love and lose again.
What joy it is to give birth to healthy sons,
to play with them, sing to them, to see them
grow in strength, acquire a warrior's skills
ready to take on a world of enemies.
What's wrong with us? Why do we not start weeping
as soon as we see the newborn's genitals?
But no, we glow with pride – as if this creature,
these perfect arms and legs, this lusty voice,
this future food for crows, were an achievement.
Brood-mares for corpses – that's what women are
if they are born accursed kshatriyas!

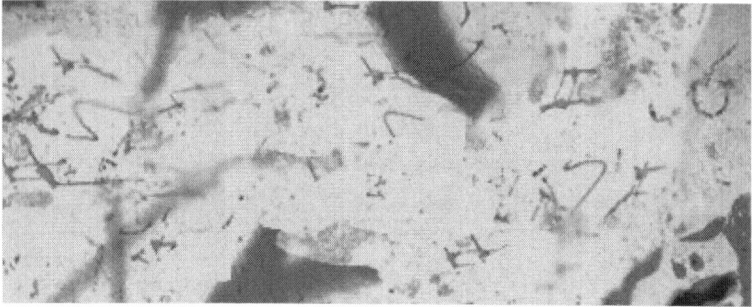

Annemarie Austin
'Come the Thaw'

(Before the advent of polar exploration it was thought that speech would freeze in very cold climates. Variations of this conceit are found in Rabelais, Castiglione, Donne and Addison.)

We would never go into those icy places,
never swing towards the pole like
a compass needle. We know how
it is: there could be no living
there, words freezing as they
left our lips, freezing and
falling to the ground to
lie like crystallized
sweets till the
thaw came.

When we might not be by to hear them.
We could not wait by our pile of words like
a cold campfire through midwinter, for we'd
freeze into pillars and trees not otherwise
to be seen in the icy places. Those
sweets would lie till there might
be a passer-by to take up one
or two and warm them in his
fingers. Then he'd hear
a word or two from
before the thaw.
              More probably the words would go
tumbling under the polar winds, jumbling into
nonsensical sentences. They'd spill across
the ground, spelling nothing said before
and melting out of order to tell
opposing stories. How could we
live like that: more than
half a year dumb, then
when the thaw comes –
knee deep in noise
and no solution.

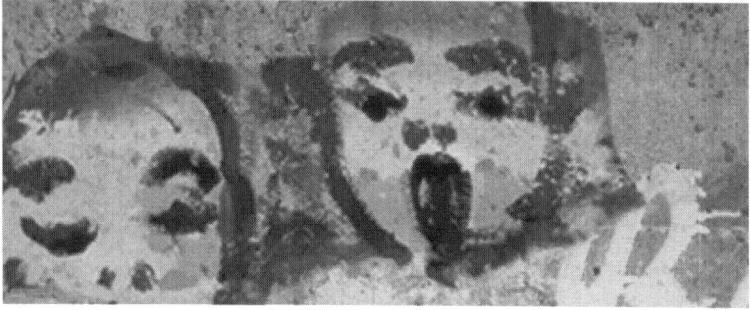

F. Mehrban
Two Poems
Translated by the author and Helen Smith

F. Mehrban is a former political prisoner from Iran who sought asylum in this country in 2002 and is now a resident and a UK citizen. She had several poems and short stories published in Iran and, after recovering from her ordeal in prison, she is now starting to write in English as well as translating some of her poems and a novel from Farsi into English. We met earlier this year when I became her writing mentor in a therapeutic writing group called Write to Life run by the Medical Foundation for the Care of Victims of Torture.

The two poems 'Remember Me' and 'Leila', were written in Farsi in memory of F. Mehrban's younger brother, Feridoon, who died after eight years in prison in Iran. Feridoon was a big fan of Pink Floyd and a line from their song, 'Wish You Were Here', is quoted in 'Remember Me'. Feridoon was engaged to a girl called Leila, his sweetheart who waited for him while he was in prison but who was eventually persuaded by her family to marry someone else shortly before he died. It must have been clear by then that there was no hope of his release but F.Mehrban's family was heart-broken.

The poems were translated from Farsi into English by F.Mehrban and I have helped her polish them.

Helen Smith

Remember Me

(*To my hero, Feridoon*)

When you see a big tree broken by a storm and fallen on the
    land
When you see a spring that has turned in on itself to form a
    lagoon
When your heart is full of the pain of injustice but your lips
    are sewn
When you're tired of solitude and loneliness
Remember me
If nobody hears your cries for justice, or hears and ignores you
    anyway
If hurt and cold and hunger prevail
As you writhe in pain at the inexorable whip
But your pride doesn't let you cry
Remember me
If you sit all day long in the dark, thinking and thinking
Darkness behind you and, in front of you, annihilation
Without a friend to remember the past
Suffering in a continual nightmare
Seeing everything dimly
Waiting for years and years to see a passer-by
Through your small window, hoping for any short message
Losing your youth
Without any pleasure
Remember me

I watered freedom's tree with my blood
But instead, I saw oppression growing
I watched the thunderstorms through the window
I heard the raindrops on the roof
But I wanted to see the drops on the flower petals in our
    garden
I heard birdsong at dawn
But I wanted to see the birds flying in the blue sky
And one day I knew that although they'd imprisoned me
They couldn't control my dreams
Then, in my small, damp cell, I dragged my wounded body
    to the darkest part of it
In my dream I made myself free
In my mind I created the voice of the wind scuffling and
    streams tumbling
I saw birds flying in the blue sky
I rode for hours and hours on my red bike
I put my head on our father's shoulder
I even smelled our mother's roses
Yes . . . I was free

Darling, remember life is magnificent when
In the middle of a rainy night, in the dark, wet streets, you
    see two lovers walking
When you pass a garden and see a small sparrow with a
    broken wing, take it
In your palm. Stroke it, mend its wings and help it fly
Fly beside it and feel free, with your whole body, then . . .
Remember me

On the big oak in the corner of our garden, carve my name
Close your eyes and imagine me beside you
Feel my arm around your shoulder
Listen... Pink Floyd are singing . . . *I wish . . . I wish you were*
    here
Turn it up loud
Think of me

Leila

You and I were two pigeons in the wide sky
We flew with the wind
Sat on the cloud's wing
Pecked at the raindrops
We were two small fish in the big ocean
Played hide and seek behind the jellyfish
Startled shellfish from their sweet sleep
Burst the water's bubbles
All night long we lay beneath the naked sky and counted the
    stars
And I made a necklace of them, for you
Hummed old love songs to put you to sleep
When dawn came, I drenched your eyelashes with the
    flowers' dew
Without you my poetry was defective
My painting hadn't any colour
But . . .
I was made of light and you of dust
I became lighter and lighter
I climbed
Separated from you
I began my lonely journey, passing the many-coloured lights
On the sky's roof I waited for you for days and days
And when I heard you'd gone with another
My happiness had the flavour of tears
But I know you'll come one day
Because without me you, too, are incomplete

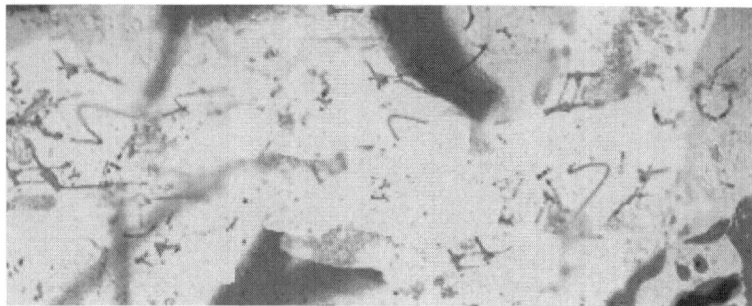

Seamus Heaney
Three 'Freed Speeches' from *Aeneid* VI

1. Aeneas
(lines 42-76)

At Cumae, behind the broad cliff, an enormous cave
Has been quarried: a hundred entrances, a hundred
Wide open mouths lead in, and out of them scramble
A hundred echoing voices, the Sibyl's reponses.
When they arrived at that threshold, the vestal cried,
'Now! Now you must ask what your fate is. The god
Is here with us! Apollo!' Her countenance suddenly
Convulsed and changed colour, hair got dishevelled,
Breast was a-heave, heart beating wilder and wilder.
Before their eyes she grows tall, something not mortal
Enters, she is changed by the breath of the god
Breathing through her. 'Aeneas of Troy,' she demands,
'Your vows and your prayers, why do you wait? Pray,
For until you have prayed, the jaws of this cavern

Won't echo or open.' And there she fell silent.
The hardy Trojans feel a cold shiver go through them,
Their prince from the depths of his heart beseeches
The god:
                'Phoebus, you always had pity for Troy
And her troubles, it was you who steadied
Paris's aim and directed the arrow
Into Achilles, it was you in the lead
As I entered sea after sea, skirting the coasts
Of distant land masses, remotest Massylia,
The sandbanked Syrtian gulfs. Here then at last
We set foot on Italia that seemed for so long
The unreachable: henceforth let Trojan ill-fortune
Be a thing of the past. For now, all you gods
And goddesses, you to whom Troy's name and fame
Gave affront, divine law constrains you
To spare us, the last of its relicts. And you,
Seeress most holy, to whom the future lies open,
Grant what I ask (no more in the end than my fate
Has assigned): home ground for my people
In Latium, refuge for our wandering gods
And all Troy ever held sacred. Then to Phoebus
Apollo and Diana I will set up a temple
In solid marble and inaugurate feast days
In the god's honour. And for you, O all gracious one,
A sanctuary will be established, a vault
Where I shall preserve divinations from lots
And oracles you'll have vouchsafed to my people,
And in your service I shall ordain chosen men.
Yet one thing I ask of you: not to inscribe
Your visions in verse on the leaves
In case they go frolicking giddily off
In the wind. Chant them yourself, I beseech you.'
So saying, Aeneas fell silent.

2. The Sibyl

(lines 77-97)

                                        Meanwhile the Sibyl
Resisting possession, storms through the cavern,
Hard put to wrestle off Phoebus Apollo
And throw him. But the more she froths at the mouth
And contorts, the more he controls her, commands her
And makes her his creature. Then of their own accord
Those hundred vast tunnel-mouths gape and give vent
To the prophetess's responses:
                                        'O you who survived,
In the end, the sea's dangers (though worse still await
On the land), you and your Trojans will come
Into the realm of Lavinium: have no fear of that.
But the day is one you will rue. I see wars,
Atrocious wars, and the Tiber surging with blood.
A second Simois river, a second Xanthus,
A second enemy camp lie ahead. And already
In Latium a second Achilles comes forth, he too
The son of a goddess. Nor will Trojans ever be free
Of Juno's harassments, while you, without allies,
Dependent, will go through Italia petitioning
Cities and peoples. And again the cause of such pain
And disaster for Trojans will be as before: a bride
Culled in a host country, an outlander groom.
But whatever disasters befall, do not flinch.
Go all the bolder to face them, follow your fate
To the limit. A road will open to safety
From the last place you would expect: a city of Greeks.'

3. Anchises

(lines 847-54)

'Others, I have no doubt, with more delicate touch
Will beat bronze into breathing likenesses,
Conjure living features out of marble,
Argue cases more effectively, and with their compass
Plot the heavens' orbit and predict
The rising of the constellations. But you, Roman,
Remember: to you will fall the exercise of power
Over the nations, and these will be your gifts –
To impose peace and justify your sway,
Spare those you conquer, crush those who overbear.'

Archilochus
'The Cologne Epode'
Translated by William Heath

Archilochus of Paros was born around 700 B.C. Ancient criticism ranked him, along with Homer, as one the greatest of poets, though many also disapproved of his frankness and sensuality. But today almost all of his work is lost. In common with most of the lyric poets of the following two centuries the manuscript tradition broke off at some point in late antiquity.

The possible reasons for this have been hotly debated by scholars and literary critics; some claiming deliberate destruction under clerical influence, others offering the more prosaic explanation that the dialects in which lyric poetry was written were simply not understood anymore, and of little use for schoolroom exercise. However it may be, the lack of interest demonstrated by Christian Byzantium in preserving the wealth of Greek lyric poetry has undoubtedly robbed us of a glorious legacy.

In the twentieth century, however, archaeology has greatly increased the number of fragments that we possess, which were previously restricted to incidental quotations in Hellenistic grammatical works. Digging in the sands of Egypt at sites such as Oxyrhynchus, English and German archaeologists revealed masses of tattered papyrus, ranging from the merest household chit to previously unknown fragments of literary works by Sappho, Sophocles and many others.

In 1974, R. Merkelbach and M.L. West published in *Zeitschrift für Papyrologie und Epigraphik,* a long fragment of one of Archilochus' Epodes from the Cologne Papyrus collection. It was one of the most remarkable finds of the century, both for its length and for the quality of the poetry. The papyrus on which it was written had been used as wrapping for a mummy, but now, more than a millennium and a half later, that papyrus has restored to us a masterpiece of ancient poetry for our study and enjoyment.

The text I follow is that found in The Loeb Classical Library's *Greek Iambic Poetry* by Douglas E. Gerber.

Behind the poem is a story, true or not, that Lycambes promised his daughter Neobule to Archilochus in marriage, then broke his word. Here Archilochus consoles himself with 'another' and heaps insults on Neobule.

The Cologne Epode

'. . . But though limb-loosening Eros shakes me,

I must beg you to go no further, and if you're
Willing to endure this fever
Then I'm certain that I can do the same.

But if you feel compelled by the Goddess, and can't
Wait one moment more, there's still a
Girl at our house whom once you suffered for;

A beautiful, slender sweetheart, quite perfect to
My young eye, why not visit with
Us again and make her your friend once more?'

Such were the words she spoke, and I made this reply:
'Dear daughter of Amphimedo,
As wise a woman as the dark earth holds,

They say golden Cypris has many delights for
Men, when the sacred act is out
Another'll have to do; you and I

Could discuss these things till the shadows start to fall,
I call all the gods as witness
That I'll follow your every word, and make

My way through the gates in the garden and bide my
Sweet time in there, but I'll pull out
When the time comes, on my honour, I swear.

But as for Neobule, let some other try,
Why should I waste time on her? She's
Nearly twice your age; an over-ripened

Peach, now her girlhood's lost its flower, the power
She once had's all but drained away,
They say that she's insatiable and I

Saw it for myself, it'll serve the crazy bitch
Right to be left up on the shelf.
For I hope that no real friend would wish

Such a wife on me, giving my cruel neighbours
An endless source of glee, I should
Much prefer that you were to be the one.

For you are not a two-faced hag, nor a silly
Precipitous witch, taking on
So many lovers so she can ape the

Proverbial bitch, I didn't want babies born
Blind and premature, but if one
Rushes on in haste nothing is so sure.'

There I left off speaking and took her by the hand,
And laid her down in the blooming
Flowers, wrapped in my woollen cloak, and as

I stroked her slender neck she gave up the struggle.
She lay trembling just like a
Fawn, but as I'd sworn I touched her gently,

Running soft hands over beautiful breasts; the rest
Of her body shone as I bared
It, new blossoming in glorious prime.

I took my time and caressed her all over, and
Stayed as long as I dared, then let
My white force loose, still touching golden hairs.

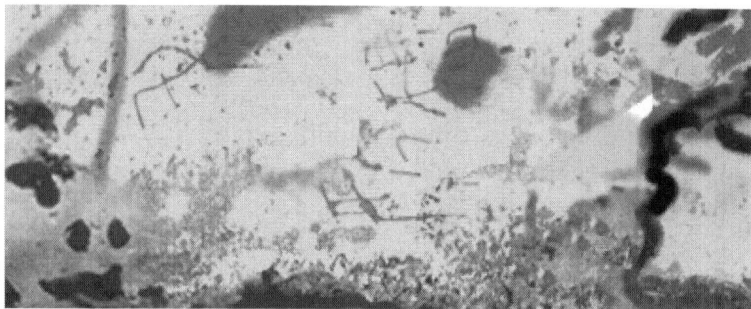

Sappho
Fragment 58
Translated by John Morey

Fleeing   5
was bitter.
You of many names:
the Muses,
deep-browed,
prosper the mouth,   10
give gifts of beauty, children.
Tuneful player of the clear-toned lyre,
old age already withers all the skin,
and turns the hair to white from black:
the knees don't carry you   15
to dance like young fawns.
There: but what to do? —
not possible – becoming ageless. –
... Rose-armed Ayos,
carry me to the end of the land.   20
—'Thus he was seized by age',
his deathless bedfellow
thinks.
They might give steel,
but *I* love delicacy, beauty; and, for me   25
love's lucked upon the brightness of the sun.

Note

I deliberately chose one of the more fragmented records of Sappho's work because I reasoned that its broken beauty in the Greek lent itself to having a new coherency by the imposition of the more flexible language of modern English. The result is a second poem, which finds modernity in this fractured syntax, while – as far as possible – being true to Sappho's palette of meanings, keeping the well-preserved and clearly translatable verbs and nouns in their original places, but adding and altering some punctuation and imposing grammar where none can be meaningfully extrapolated from these traces. So, taking these fragments of lines, I think that I have freed the disjointed vestiges of this untitled piece of seventh-century Greek lyric poetry from incomprehensibility. While I know there is discussion over papyri, I have worked from the Oxyrhynchus papyrus, this being the first that I encountered. I consider my piece as much a poem as a translation. Having included lines 23-6 I was reluctant to omit them, since they are, I think, the most beautiful.

(Fragment 58)

$$
\begin{array}{lll}
&]ύγοισα[\quad] & 5 \\
]\,.\,[\,.\,.\,]\,.\,.\,[\quad]ιδάχθην & \\
]χυ\ θ[\,\acute{.}\,]ο\iota[\,.\,]αλλ[\ldots\ldots]ύταν & \\
]\,.\,χθο.[\,\acute{.}\,]ατί\,.\,[\ldots\ldots]εισα & \\
]μένα\ ταν[\ldots\ldots ώ]νυμόν\ σε & \\
]νι\ θῆται\ στ[ύ]μα[τι]\ πρόκοψιν & 10 \\
]πων\ κάλα\ δῶρα\ παῖδές & \\
]φιλάοιδον\ λιγύραν\ χελύνναν & \\
πά]ντα\ χρόα\ γῆρας\ ἤδη & \\
λεῦκαι\ δ'\ ἐγένο]ντο\ τρίχες\ ἐκ\ μελαίναν & \\
]αι,\ γόνα\ δ'\ [ο]ὐ\ φέροισι & 15 \\
]ησθ'\ ἴσα\ νεβρίοισιν & \\
ἀ]λλὰ\ τί\ κεν\ ποείην; & \\
]\ οὐ\ δύνατον\ γένεσθαι & \\
]\ βροδόπαχυν\ Αὔων & \\
ἔσ]χατα\ γᾶς\ φέροισα[& 20 \\
]ον\ ὔμως\ ἔμαρψε[& \\
ἀθαν]άταν\ ἄκοιτιν & \\
]ιμέναν\ νομίσδει & \\
]αις\ ὀπάσδοι & \\
ἔγω\ δὲ\ φίλημμ'\ ἀβροσύναν,\quad]τοῦτο\ καί\ μοι & 25 \\
τὸ\ λά[μπρον\ ἔρος\ τὠελίω\ καὶ\ τὸ\ κάλον & \\
\quad\quad\quad\quad λέ[λ]ογχε. & \\
\end{array}
$$

Shazea Quraishi
The Courtesan's Reply

The Courtesan's Reply is a sequence of poems inspired by M Ghosh's translation from the Sanskrit of the *Caturbhani*, four monologue plays written around 300 BC on the life of courtesans in India.

In the original plays, a narrator walks through the courtesans' quarter, commenting on the women he meets and engaging them in a one-sided conversation. I enjoyed the sensuality, charm and formality of Ghosh's prose immensely, but more than that, I was captivated by the courtesans glimpsed through the filter of the narrator. My intention was to give them a voice, and although I began by staying loyal to Ghosh's translation, I found that the courtesans wanted to say 'no, it was not like that, it was like this.'

The first two poems, 'Sixty-four Arts' and 'The Days of Chandragupta Maurya' emerged out of research into the period of the *Caturbhani*.

The Sixty-Four Arts

And so, a courtesan of pleasant disposition,
beautiful and otherwise attractive,
master of sixty-four arts including
music, dancing, acting, singing,
the composition of poetry,
flower-arrangement and garland-making,
the preparation of perfumes and cosmetics,
dress-making and embroidery,
conjuring and sleight of hand,
logic, cooking, sorcery,
fencing with sword and staff, archery,
gymnastics, carpentry,
architecture, chemistry
and minerology,
the composition of riddles,
tongue-twisters and other puzzles,
gardening, writing in cipher,
languages, making artificial flowers
and clay modelling,
training fighting cocks, partridges
and rams, and teaching parrots and mynah-birds to talk . . .
such a courtesan will be honoured by the King, praised
by the learned, and all will seek her favours
and treat her with consideration.

The Days of Chandragupta Maurya

were split into sixteen hours
of ninety minutes each.

In the first,
he arose
and prepared himself by meditation;
in the second,
he studied the reports of his agents
and issued secret instructions;
in the third,
he met with his councillors;
in the fourth,
he attended to state finances and national defence;
in the fifth,
he heard the petitions and suits of his subjects
and in the sixth,
bathed and dined and read religious literature.
He received taxes and tribute
and made official appointments in the seventh hour.
In the eighth,
he met his council again and heard
the reports of his spies and courtesans.
The ninth hour was devoted to relaxation
and prayer,
while the tenth and eleventh hours were given
to military matters
and the twelfth to secret reports.
In the thirteenth hour,
the King indulged in an evening bath and a meal,
and for the next three hours he slept
– but never in the same bed twice.

Note
CM ruled for twenty-four years. Wearying of suppressing constant revolts, and suffering from tensions and the burdens of a ruler and fear of assassination, he abdicated to become a Jain monk until he fasted to death.

Tambulasena

In the beginning
my whole body was covered with skin
hard as rock. Then he came

and his mouth was a river
running over me, cool and quick
with small, silver fish.

Night after night
he shaped me
and smoothed me

down
to my velvet
bones.

*

Now, I bathe while he watches,
feel his eyes,
fireflies on my skin.

I bend over,
my hair, a curtain of water
between us.

I let him towel me dry,
his strokes soft at first, then brisk,
like a cloth shining a lamp.

Water drips down
my back. He grasps the rope
of my hair and climbs.

Radika

Return
to me, beloved,
and take me on your lap.

Take my face
into your hands,
undo my braid, stiff

as buffalo horn
and draw your
fingers through my hair.

Untie my belt, open
the silk cloth
covering my waist,

Let my oiled limbs, my
perfumed skin
envelop you

as the rose
swallows
the bee.

Sondasi

When he stands before me
I smile slow as honey,

offer him
my pollen-dusted breasts.
I press my nose to his skin,
smell Varunika on him.
                    Wait

the word a caress,
I undress him
– the first time I have done this.

**

The next day he returns
and she is not with him.

I seat him on the low, green chair.
I move in his lap
put my mouth to his ear:
          Tell me what you do with her

He tells me
and I show him
the flame lit inside me.

**

Varunika,
queen of forests.

Her teeth marks on his lips,
          her nail marks on his back,
                    her love note to me.

**

The dark pink flower that fell
from her hair as she passed
– I hold it carefully in my hand: five petals,
one scattered with small, dark markings.
          Are there markings on her body?

Opening it, I stroke the velvet
inside, eleven stamens raise
their pollen-tipped nubs
to the tip of my tongue.

The petals droop
under the heat of my gaze,
their edges softly frilling.

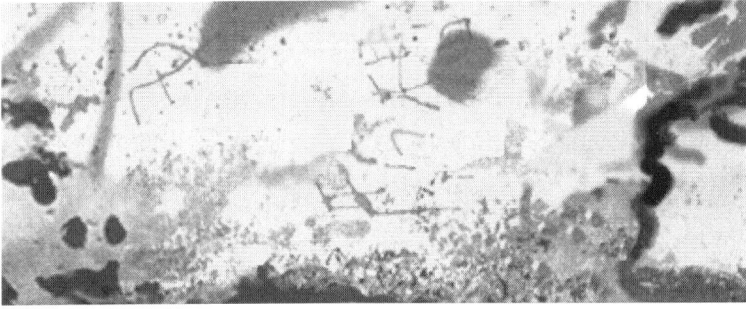

Poems from Romania
Translated by Adam Sorkin and others

Romanian literature had a history of repression under communism but, from the 1960s on, poetry seemed to occupy a somewhat privileged niche that allowed a coded, ironic, parabolic between-the-lines expression of hidden meanings. These 'lizards', as writers and readers came to call them, seemed both natural and elusive, now-you-see-them-now-you-don't sleights of the pen. Since the fall of censorship with the December 1989 revolution, minus such restrictions, poets can speak any old way. Or any new way. Some of the old ways quickly became passé but Romanian poets have flourished, exploring a wide range of stylistic possibilities and lyrical (though mainly anti-lyrical) postures.

Mircea Cărtărescu completed his manuscript *Nothing* (a bookend to his earlier collection, *Everything*) by the early 1990s but never published it, turning exclusively to prose (though he reprinted his published poetry); the poem published in this issue of *MPT* is the title poem of the volume, a kind of farewell to verse. Petre Stoica, the eldest of the group here, indulged himself in much more explicit and openly political satire, not only in his angry *Tiananmen Square II* (1991), written in reaction to the violent incursion of the miners into Bucharest, but also *The Master of the Hunt Visits* (2002); Romanian readers would remember in a flash that the dictator Ceaușescu prided himself on his hunting prowess, though henchmen did the shooting for him. Ioan Flora brings as acerbic an irony and a similar sense of surrealism to his otherwise rather different poetry; born in Serbia across the border from Romania, Flora spoke to me about *Medea and Her War Machines* (in which he published 'Parallel Worlds') as a kind of parable of human impulses toward war, vengeance and violence in 'an old and tragic story in which history becomes a web of flesh'. Marta Petreu, inevitably outspoken and recognizable in her strong, powerfully rhetorical literary voice and her politically engaged scholarship and editing, writes as a woman arguing with God as if eternity's dictator and the failed, egotistical creator of a flawed world of death and human subservience. Floarea Ţuţuianu's poetry has been described to me by a Romanian poet-friend as 'sexy'; certainly there is no communist-period prurience in her poetical art, which she began to write and publish only after 1990 (these poems would not have been passed by the Socialist Republic's censor). Dan Sociu, the youngest writer among these – I first met him in the 1990s in Iaşi when he was a young university student – has to many Romanian critics become the most prominent member of the varied writers whose biographical self-projection and depiction of life is usually characterized as *miserabilism*. Sociu's energy and gifts transcend mere wallowing in depression and defeatism, but when I hear the term, I'm amused to call to mind the requisite positivist and progressive attitudes of the 'proletcultist' ideals and literary constrictions of the Stalinist period that began what is often spoken of as the Romanians' 'forty years' war' against ideological control.

Adam J. Sorkin

Mircea Cărtărescu
'Nothing'
Translated by Adam Sorkin and Daniel Mangu

Mircea Cărtărescu is Romania's most celebrated writer among
the self-conscious postmodernists of the 1980s – the 'blue-jeans
generation'. He published six collections of poetry before turning
to prose fiction and essays. His novel *Nostalgia* was published by
New Directions; the first two volumes of his major work, *Orbitor*,
will appear as *Dazzler* from the University Press of Plymouth.

Nothing

fuck depression!
I've had it with begging for compassion!
with being in charge of the union's operation!
with always being nagged, 'hurry, write! hurry, orate!'
concentrate, you s.o.b.!
create, create, create!
davai, davai! don't stop! a novel a year till you drop!
get yourself in gear and keep it up,
to remain among the living here,
to make a place for sure in the history of literature!
to be worthy of our culture!

I've had it with feeling bad after I've written!
with feeling bad after I've not written!
with your staring at me as if I were the walking dead
whenever I haven't spewed forth pages or read!
maybe my brain's sick and tired
of you; of everything and everybody – all this shit!
It's possible I've glimpsed your sagging tit
when I lit the lamp in the bedroom,
your rhymestress's literary fit!

it's too much! it's driven me mad!
my brain's fallen apart, gone bad,
the God who used to provide light and an answer
lately has contracted oesophageal cancer.
I don't want to cross that threshold!
I've written poetry for fifteen years
and today everyone sneers and jeers,
literature's illiterates, ill-willed scribblers,
once friends, now pissers, ass-kissers!

davai, davai! you wouldn't give a damn if I just upchuck!
cărtărescu's plumb out of luck!
we're rescued from an obsession!
may he rest in peace!
it's his fault we couldn't recover from our disaster!
third-rate poetaster!
in his latest book at long last it's obvious
that all this time he's been worthless beyond repair!
a bicycle pump has puffed him up with air!

> . . . and perhaps it's true . . .
> . . . the devil knows, perhaps it's true . . .

anyhow, I want you to know that I don't give two sous.
I no longer even peek at my reviews
I don't visit anyone to gossip about news
I won't write even a letter.
I am truly at peace!
my life hasn't ceased and I feel much better.

Ioan Flora
'Parallel Worlds'
Translated by Adam Sorkin and Alina Cârâc

Ioan Flora (1950–2005), author of fifteen books of poetry, among them *Lecture on the Ostrich-Camel* (1995), *The Swedish Rabbit* (1998), *Medea and Her War Machines* (2000), died just days after his last book, *Luncheon Under the Grass*, was launched. Born in Yugoslavia in the Romanian-speaking region of the Serbian Banat across the border from Romania, Flora lived in Bucharest from the early 1990s.

Parallel Worlds

to George Astalos

For more than a century, I've been propped on the pediment of the Hôtel de Ville,
to catch my breath, smoke a cigarette, leaf through
the pages of the catalogue of Brâncuşi's studios.

Concrete data, everyday places – ultimately useful.
More gripping are the video images (more startling)
from the precincts of the white dwelling;
the bustle of a Gorj farmyard in the sixties,
milking sheep,
herding cattle to pasture,
the gimpy-legged farmhand from the collective limping up
    the steps of the watermill,
slaughtering a pig at the gate.

Compelling images that feature country people:
covered with green tectonic plates, blinking with
bloodshot eyes,
tomorrow already
in tatters, a day of blue vitriol.
And if I also take heed of the work song scouring
every nook of the studio, if I keep in mind
the perfume of the *Songs of the Prison Camps*
('Pandele didn't miss a beat, caught me trying to cheat –
from up my sleeve, a royal flush; hey ho! I didn't even blush.'
'The strife I've been through in this life!'
'Bring me my Adidas, Ma, I'm heading out the door!'),
I could speak of the deceitful existence
of parallel worlds,
I could even let day darken to black
(with abstract pain, with mindless fury),
and the vault might collapse, earth and all that is,
into the coffee cup on the table.

August light in September.
Propped on the pediment of the Hôtel de Ville.
Staples for the stapler.
Blueberries for blueberry wine.
Ambulances, the pulse of emergency lights, public order
profaning the disquiet of this Thursday.
Parallel worlds, superfluous prayers.

Paris, 9 September 1998

Marta Petreu
'The Last Judgement'
Translated by Adam Sorkin

Marta Petreu published *Bring Verbs* in 1981, which won the Romanian Writers' Union Prize for a first volume. She has issued six other collections, including *Jacob's Ladder*. In 2001, she was awarded a Hellman/Hammett Grant from Human Rights Watch. Petreu, also a philosopher, and scholar, is a founder and editor of one of the most outspoken magazines of post-communist Romania, *Apostrof*.

The Last Judgement

We are the abyss we are truth we are arrogance
we ride horses without reins the great horses of the final days
red dark shrieking
like your horde of man-eating angels

We understand we know we won't restrain ourselves
we are no longer afraid of you

and we no longer glorify you

We are truth your many-headed whore
we judge you: we will be just with your world
your slapdash world
You cannot be forgiven. You cannot be forgotten. We saddle
the great horses we pass judgement

We – the mortals

We chant:
O Lord, take back your keys
the keys of your kingdom of sickness death garbage
the keys of your butcher shop on earth
take them back, O Glorious Lord

We – the mortals

Dan Sociu
'I say love in a language . . .'
Translated by Adam Sorkin and the poet with Mihaela Niță

Dan Sociu's third book of poetry, *eXcessive songs* (2005), won the Romanian Writers' Union Prize for the best poetry book of the year – the first time a book by a non-member was either nominated or won this major prize. In 2008, his first novel, *Urbancolia*, was published to acclaim. He has translated Charles Bukowski into Romanian.

I say love in a language . . .

I say love in a language
taught with interdictions
I write love with lumps in my throat
a towering woman
watches me
crushes my knuckles
with an iron ruler
love

thrown out of the house
you know love
only as an escape from home
you pant underneath me
as if it were a race
and at the end
there's nothing
waiting for you no one
not even me
you whisper love with lumps in your throat
trembling you listen
how your home
pounds at the door
their love is threatening
they'll drag us by the hair
naked out on the staircase
they'll talk about us in their language
our love language

Petre Stoica
Three poems
Translated by Adam Sorkin and Ioana Ieronim

Petre Stoica (1931–2009) has been publishing books since 1957,
with more than twenty volumes to his name. A major translator
of German-language poetry, he has won numerous Romanian
literary awards. Often satiric and playful in his poems, Stoica's
literary stature has been growing over the past two decades. He
died in March 2009.

after the fog thickened

a heavy fog
embraced the land

the messengers entrusted with the good news
got lost and wound up in another country

after the fog thickened
we no longer could recognize each other

we all became
democratic deaf-mutes

news flash

archaeologists have discovered
new indigenous virtues

we're going to have worldwide media coverage
scholarly symposia the awarding
of academic titles

our higher authorities
will partake in a banquet
with all manner of seafood and ram's balls
in a sauce of violets

on the internet they'll post
the musical scores of gravelly speeches

the master of the hunt visits

gracefully the train glides into the station festooned
with garlands of braided wild boars' ears

ave ave the multitude of beaters thunder out
ave ave reply the piccolos of disinfected heavens

the mayor holds out bread and salt to welcome the master of
     the hunt
in his excitement the mayor's solemn beard falls off

the choir of fashion models hired by the hour
intones lauds for the hunters fallen in the line of duty

the procession heads to where in adherence to
the most recent canon of postmodern art
a vast bald-eagle preserve will be located

the master of the hunt straightens his tie patriotically
he speaks about the abnegation of simple hunters
about the impediments to hunting in stormy weather
he speaks about poaching by strangers
they join in condemnation ask for vigilance at the
     watchtowers

ave ave the multitude of beaters thunder out
while the honoured guest the master of the hunt
visits the old people's home
doles out apples aspirin and advice
and for those who are hobbled by gout
leads Viennese waltz lessons

ave ave the ovations resound to the ends of the night
multiplied far beyond
the frontiers of this rheumatic season

Floarea Ţuţuianu
Two poems
Translated by Adam Sorkin and Irma Giannetti

Floarea Ţuţuianu, a visual artist, graduated from the Nicolae
Grigorescu Institute of the Fine Arts in Bucharest. A graphic
designer at the Romanian Cultural Institute Publishing House
in Bucharest, she began to publish her individualistic feminist
poetry in the 1990s. Her four books of poetry include *The Lion
Mark* (2000) and *The Art of Seduction* (2002).

La femme poison

Tarted up
and dragged down by thought
secretly polishing a solitude of dreams
Yes. I'm a body who flings herself at words

The fresh smell of paper, ink
makes me giddy. When I read
I can multiply by means of spores

Pencil in my hand I caress you
and take your breath away
(so flower-like yet carnivorous)

Even now you won't leave me
with my face washed by words on the knife –
edge of the tongue –
when the last verse loses its way

Self-Portrait with Chimera

It took its time
before it its shadow
trampling it on all fours

Its face looked like a vestal virgin's
half was in the light –
(it had a sensuous mouth with a snake's
tongue, slanted nostrils and an eye
whose gaze charred everything it looked upon)
The other half of the face was
deep in shadow – a gorgon lost in thought

It had a woman's stride and a cat's gait
its nut-like sex was covered
by neither hand nor hair
but by a lion's tail or a snake's
It smelled of fetid woman
freshly possessed female

I'd have liked it beside me to get to know it
(it stretched out on its belly its face in the dust
I stretched out on my back my face in the light)
to have chatted together:
how it swallowed like swords scores of men
who didn't know what to answer –
how I gave myself to old King David
and how – nobody can ever touch me again –
and other trifles . . .
But unexpectedly it opened its eagle's
wings (unnoticed before then)
let its shadow cover me and flew
like a thought in sunlight

Marie Luise Kaschnitz
Two poems
Translated by Harry Guest

Marie Luise Kaschnitz was born in Karlsruhe in 1901. After writing two novels in the 1930s she began writing poetry. *Gedichte* appeared in 1947 followed by further collections. A firm if unorthodox Christian, she produced short stories and radio plays, dying in Rome in 1974.

Spirals

We put down words on cowhide
Who'd bother to read anything
that wasn't written on cowhide?
Five dollars for anyone who still understands our language
and will pay attention to a poem.
The rain listens
so does the indifferent sunset
That's not enough.
The dog's coat bristles

he shivers and howls near the ford
That's not enough.
The dreamer tumbles from the roof
He went spiralling down
Whorled ammonite for a gravestone
That's enough.

Unsaid

Unsaid
whatever there was to say about the sun
and the truth about lightning
not to speak of love

Attempts. Petitions. Failed.

Daybreak let go of
No mention of the sower
And nothing noticed by the path except
one buttercup and a violet

Your backbone unbraced
by eternal salvation
Decay not gainsaid
nor despair

Satan not pushed to the wall
since I don't believe in him
God not praised
but then who am I that

Copyright of the German originals of both poems: Insel Verlag
Frankfurt am Main, 1985

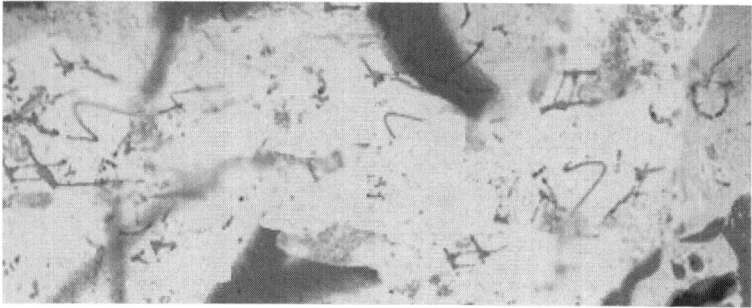

Amit Chaudhuri
'The Writers'
(On constantly mishearing 'rioting' as 'writing' on the BBC)

There has been writing for ten days now
unabated. People are anxious, fed up.
There is writing in Paris, in disaffected suburbs,
but also in small towns, and old ones like Lyon.
The writers have been burning cars; they've thrown
homemade Molotov cocktails at policemen.
Contrary to initial reports, the writers
belong to several communities: Algerian
and Caribbean, certainly, but also Romanian,
Polish, and even French. Some are incredibly
young: the youngest is thirteen.
They stand edgily on street-corners, hardly
looking at each other. Long-standing neglect
and an absence of both authority and employment
have led to what are now ten nights of writing.

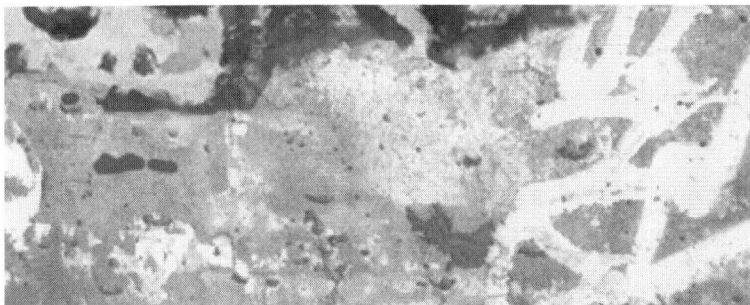

Jazra Khaleed
Three poems
Translated by Peter Constantine

Jazra Khaleed was born in Grozny, Chechnya, in 1979. Today he lives in Athens, writes and publishes exclusively in Greek, and is known as a boxer and poet. He is among the first of a new generation of Athenian writers born beyond the borders of Greece, with roots in other cultures and languages, bringing to Greek poetry an un-Greek linguistic and poetic energy. Khaleed has drawn a parallel between boxing and poetry: his writing has the attack and punch of the fighter. Much of his poetry is an indictment of the oppression of the people in Chechnya, and the harsh lot of the immigrant in a Greece that offers few opportunities to outsiders. He has in fact remained an outsider to Greek literary circles, unpublished by the mainstream Greek publishers and literary magazines. He has circulated his poetry in samizdat and online, and in the new wave magazine *Teflon*, where he now also works as an editor and translator of German, American and Australian poetry.

Self-portrait

Happiness knocked on my window this morning
Diamonds around her neck
I looked the other way
Turned my back on her
Spoke harsh words
No, I won't turn murderer on her account

Every morning I eat pain with my cornflakes
Every evening I challenge my sanity
I want to turn into summer
To run naked on the beach
Admired by all

God is a worthy comrade
He prays to me
Partakes of my body
Drinks of my blood
At times he sits at my feet
I run my fingers through his hair

Cares, qualms, compassion mean nothing to me
Every Sunday I read funeral orations in churches
I'm sorry, but I don't take requests
Whenever I hear the word peace
I sleep with a gun under my pillow

Jazra Khaleed is my name
A holy whore
A bastard poet
A fighter sometimes, mostly a coward
I know who I am
I have stained the honour of every honourable family
I've laid every talk-show hostess
Similes are my strongpoint
I've collected curses from every cursed poet

Show me a woman and I will impregnate her
Or a sun and I will darken it
Give me a fatherland and I will betray it
Or assassinate its tyrant
Expose its president
Book me at a circus
Or an international poetry festival
Swear at me, spit at me, and I will crucify myself for your
     pleasure
Teach me foreign tongues and touch-typing
Force me to read newspapers and watch television
Teach me sweet-talk and flattery
Poets, too, need to be useful in some way

I write in the name of all vagrants, barefoot indigents,
Those who are last
As I roll on the sidewalk and throw up outside bars
This is the only worthy cause

I am a promise that nobody will keep

Death Tonight

Tonight death will turn widower
Machine guns still lusting in heat
Soldiers return to their countries
Castrated
Maimed
No longer to shoot
No longer to rape
Death sticks to their fingers like resin
Their deaths
The days stop at a checkpoint
The days are Moslem mothers
They don't have papers, they are deported
Tonight death will turn widower
I saw peace pluck her eyebrows
Just before she stepped on stage
Chewing popcorn
The masses on the square
Applaud the bombing of innocents
Murders of immigrants
The victory of civilization
The triumph of democracy
A first-world strip show
Tonight death will turn widower
Shrieks of dishonoured women deafen my ears
Cluster bombs burrow into my stomach
I rule the moon
I assign all ebb and flow
The cops try to imprison gravity
Yet another undeclared war
The children's eyes shine black in the Apache's searchlights
Filled with ashes
Filled with hatred
Remorseless
Oblivion is selling one more genocide on eBay
Tomorrow is already a word without future
Death tonight

Intro

I have no people
The rats you keep chew at my lips
My solitude is like a sharpened razorblade
It grazes your naked carotids
Gillette's my sponsor
Don't mistake me for a Saturday
I'm simply a fucked-up Tuesday
Without sun
Without rain
But with breasts full of milk
My head filled with words
Against heads filled with coins
Follow me
If you want to see your face on YouTube
But I want you to know
That I wrote these words with my bare hands
In a world ruled by eyes
I sprained my middle finger
Trying to write out a list of everyone I hate
But I want you to know
That I wrote this poem with my bare hands
On the neck of my boss
Little boys in the street will call out my name
Jazra Khaleed: poetry whore
My name was Panayiotis – Holy of Holies – how disgusting
I wanted to wash from my body the white male's shame
But allow me to keep
A little of a good Christian's barbarity – a down payment
I am Jazra
Roughneck poet
Known unknown
Proletarian immigrant
Son of a Moslem mother
Father to none
      Who are you?

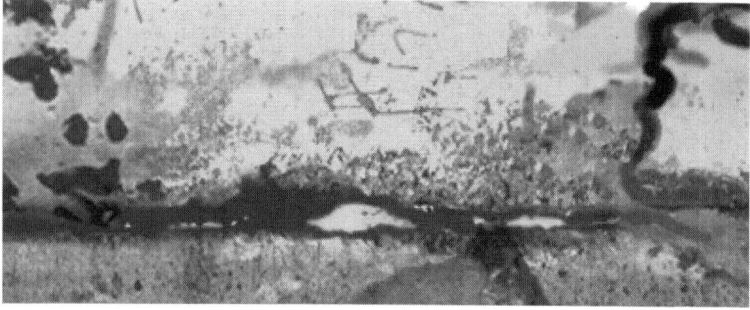

Mangalesh Dabral
Three poems
Translated by Sudeep Sen

Mangalesh Dabral (born in 1948) has published five collections of poems in Hindi: *Pahar Par Laltein* (Lantern on Mountain, 1981), *Ghar Ka Rasta* (The Way Home, 1981), *Hum Jo Dekhate Hain* (That Which We See, 1995), *Aawaaz Bhi Ek Jagah Hai* (Voice Too is a Place, 2000), *Mujhe Dikha Ek Manushya* (I saw a Human Being, 2008); and three collections of prose: *Ek Baar Iowa* (Once upon Iowa, travel diary, 1996), *Lekhak Ki Roti* (Writer's Bread, cultural essays, 1998), and *Kavi Ka Akelapan* (Poet's Solitude, 2008). His poems have appeared in *Periplus, Atlas, Gestures* and *Signatures, Modern Poetry in Translation, Poetry Review* and *Europa*. His awards include: the Sahitya Akademi Award, Sahityakar Samman, and Pahal Samman. Dabral lives in New Delhi and works with National Book Trust.

Accompanist

Accompanying the main singer's monolith-weighed voice
His own is beautiful delicate and quavering
He is the singer's younger brother
Or his apprentice
Or a distant relative who travels on foot to learn
Under the main singer's baritone
He matches his own echo since old times
Singing the second verse through tone's intricate jungle
Lost in the scale's unstruck note
Straying into the scale's further reaches
It is the accompanist who keeps the theme steady
Like gathering up the main singer's left-behind objects
Like reminding him of his childhood
When he was just a novice
In the higher registers when the singer's voice gives way
Inspiration leaving him fervour fading
His voice shedding ash-like
It is then that blending with the main singer
Appears from somewhere the accompanist's tone
Sometimes he simply sings to join in
To remind the singer that he is not alone
And that once again the song can be sung
The same *raga* that has already been sung
And in his voice the faltering that is audible
Or his voice's attempt at not raising the high notes
This shouldn't be taken as his incompetence
But his own humanity.

Touch

Touch the things that are kept on the table in front of you
Clock pen-stand an old letter
Idol of Buddha Bertolt Brecht and Che Guevara's photos
Open the drawer and touch its old sadness
Touch a blank sheet of paper with the words' fingers
Touch like a pebble the still water of a van Gogh painting
Starting life's hullabaloo in it
Touch your forehead and hold it for a long while without
     feeling shame
To touch it isn't necessary for someone to sit close
From very far it is possible to touch even
Like a bird from a distance who keeps her eggs protected

'Please do not touch' or 'Touching is prohibited' don't believe
     in such phrases
These are long-running conspiracies
Religious-gurus holding flags wearing crowns and shawls
Bomb-throwers, war-raisers indulge in for keeping us apart
The more dirt the more waste they spit
Only by touch can they be cleansed
Touch you must even though it turns things topsy-turvy
Don't touch the way gods priests bigots devotees disciples
Touch each others' feet and heads
Rather touch the way the tall grass appears to caress the
     moon and stars
Go inward feel the moist spot touch
See if it still remains there or not in these ruthless times.

This Number Does Not Exist

This number does not exist.
Wherever I go whichever number I dial
At the other end a strange voice says
This number does not exist *yeh number maujood nahin hai*
Not too long ago at this number I used to reach people
Who said: of course we recognize you
There is space for you in this universe

But now this number does not exist it is some old number.
At these old addresses very few people are left
Where at the sound of footsteps doors would be opened
Now one has to ring the bell and wait in apprehension
And finally when one appears
It is possible that he might have changed
Or he might say I am not the one you used to talk to
This is not the number where you would hear out your grief

Wherever I go numbers maps faces seem to be changed
Old diaries are strewn in the gutters
Their names slow-fading in the water
Now other numbers are available more than ever with and
    without wires
But a different kind of conversation on them
Only business only transactions buy-and-sell voices like
    strangers
Whenever I go I desperately dial a number
And ask for the voice that used to say
The door is open you can stay here
Come along for a while just for the sake of it any time in this
    universe.

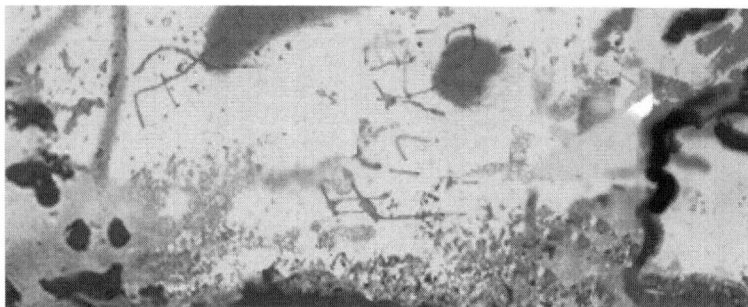

Pawlo Tychyna
Six poems
Translated by Steve Komarnyckyj

Pawlo Tychyna and the Executed Renaissance

Pawlo Tychyna (1891–1967) is the most significant member of a generation of writers who would come to be known as 'the Executed Renaissance' after the anthology compiled by Yuri Lavrinenko and published in Paris in 1959. These authors enjoyed considerable creative freedom in the 1920s as the Soviet Regime sought to secure the loyalty of the Ukrainian population by encouraging the development of Ukrainian culture. Unfortunately Stalin, who was wary of Ukraine's growing assertiveness and independence, sought, as Rafael Lemkin noted, to destroy the nation by means of a policy of genocide aimed at the Ukrainian farmer and the country's spiritual, political and cultural elite. During the 1930s 226 of 253 Ukrainian writers were executed or rendered inactive by the Soviet Police. They died in the underground basements of police stations, in Arctic labour camps, they were shot and tortured, they died of hypothermia, exhaustion, malnutrition. Tychyna was one of the few surviving members of this talented generation of authors. The price he paid for his survival was writing ream after ream of Stalinist doggerel.

I Wept

The storm clouds assemble
A crumbling´ relief,
The bereaved marble
And blank eyeballs of grief

Through which numb prayers pass.
A leaf falls
Onto the altar,
Wind makes the bells whisper.

Elsewhere the snow has fallen,
Where soldiers sleep
In the blank grip of stone.
Earth dreams their blurred sleep.

Though you and I are alone,
All we had once,
Wakes in the cherry's stone.
The swallow's aspiration. Spring happens.

1918

Open the Door

Open the door,
I hear his footstep
Open the door,
Only blue sky
Where a feather of cloud twists
Into emptiness.
My eyes, my heart
Turn into coral
As I wait.

Nowhere to hide
When the doors blew open,
Nowhere to lay his head
In wind and rain,
Darling, for every road
Shines with blood
And the night weeps
Empty tears
As God sleeps.

1918

What . . .

What should I say but the spring
Has opened a door in the sky
For light to pour in.
We walk through it
Soft waves, roughly knee height
Whispering.

Wrapped in a brittle silence
Until we hear the cuckoo . . .
Its two note song opens
A symphony
Through the distance we
Listen as it sings.

1918

The Spring Passes

Spring in the flex of an elm's branch
Or the chance
Dimple of water
Where the river shapes to sand and stone
Or scampers through itself laughing

Summer in the blonde or the bronze surf
Of rye,
At mid day or at dusk
As you walk by. One of the stalks perhaps
Plucked like an eyelash.

Autumn comes bereft of love
The half-formed human
Shapes of fog,
A blurred wave,
A dagger in a silk glove.

Under the snow the grass
Yellowed and numb,
Sensing the creep
Of light and shadow.
I touch her in my sleep,

Her smile a dove balancing
Her kiss a feather dancing on my lips.

1918

It Dawns

Dawn, so mellow
Has sheathed the field in a soft glow,
Poplars and golden mist
Recall coils of incense and snuffed candlewicks,
On the subtle keyboard
Of my soul. The dawn, so gentle

And quiet,
The weak stars fade into the light,
An owl calls lazily
And a grave converses with the sky,
Although it has no words
But the growing light,
Which erases the sky and wakes the birds.

The sun
Has hurt the earth alive, its wounds open,
Clouds adorn themselves with silver
And fog trembles over the field.
I run through the grass remade
Into a heaven
Beyond massacres, a burning sword.

1918

Terror

And again we must endure
Evangelist and poet
And the Philosopher who says
'Slay the sin within the flesh'

And again a dog worries at
A corpse in a heap
Of garbage.

'Each great *Idea* requires a sacrifice'
Is it a sacrifice when beast eats beast?
You with the slashed throat

When did you cease to love
In this place
Where beast eats beast eats beast . . .

1920

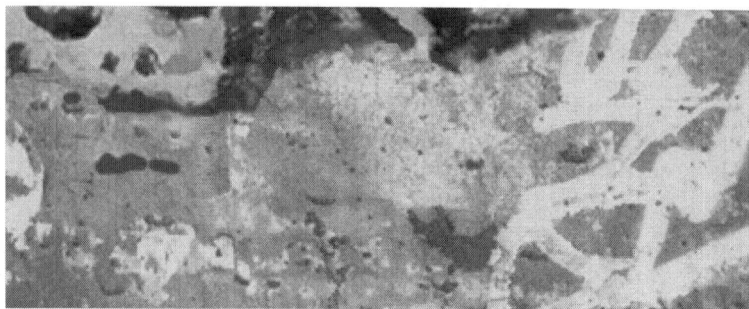

Wojciech Bonowicz
Six poems
Translated by Elżbieta Wójcik-Leese

Wojciech Bonowicz's poems celebrate freedom of speech in a quiet and unassuming fashion, at the same time not shying away from such 'big' forms as the chorus of an ancient tragedy or lament or prayer. His is a celebration of the will to speak through reflection on the repeated choruses of history, which need to be sung as much as love songs, evoking the living and the dead. Cornered by this need, the poet (or the speaker) must will the words out, under the breath, in order to breathe.

Bonowicz (b.1967) is an author of four poetry volumes; the most recent *High Seas* was awarded the prestigious Gdynia Literary Prize in 2007 (my selection is based on this book). He is also an essayist and literary critic working for one of the most influential Polish weeklies, *Tygodnik Powszechny*. His poetry samples his two strong interests: philosophy and religion, although it does not manifest them openly. His poems are not declarations of faith; nor are they easy epiphanies. Rather, they are modest, human-size, personal revelations, which frequently set off to examine our understanding of suffering, evil, death – and leave us with even more questions. It is these questions, however, that allow us empathy and transcendence of our human limitations. Like Józef Tischner, the Catholic philosopher whose biography he has prepared (it was shortlisted for the most important literary award in Poland, the Nike Prize), Bonowicz believes that 'man is the kind of tree which doesn't want to bear the fruit of evil'.

Choruses of History

They were running with torches
around the town of paper.
When they burnt the first,
I cried.

Your lips are flickering,
my love. Flickering
hoops on your neck,
paper sheet on your chest.

I have found a new name.
Wrapped it round my children.
May they run away long
through the corridors of sleep.

Silence has a heavy hand.
I will bear its grip.
As long as they are there:
the grand, joyful and evil.

Your lips are flickering,
and your forehead. Like a bird
in the night tree, my love.
Like the bodies by the river.

Pillars

Those small spirits who were to look
in the eyes of the dead. From a height
a palm tree a Doric column a stork's
nest a bean stalk. Now they avert their gaze
mysteriously holding hands above their heads.

Islands

They do not die: they arrive at the islands, dry
and flat, washed with the waters of memory.
Before the chipped goddess of judgement.
They do not suffer, nor wait,
because there will be no judgement. But justice
has left a sign.

High Seas

Yet another moment he is sitting in the warmth
among the scattered clothes.
Thinking of his father, whom he bathed here a moment ago.

Hunters

One flushes out the fish, another readies the net.
He needs to reach deep under the roots of the trees.

And if it's God and his opponent
working this afternoon together?

Night

The poem
first shuts you inside.
It doesn't want
you to look around, search
for different words
in different poems.

You sit cornered in the stone,
a scrunched
sheet of paper.
Defenceless and resigned,
you don't breathe. The poem
won't allow.

Inside the stone you can't
fidget or use
a bed a watch a map
and all the rest
of your imagination.

The poem
has its own imagination,
erected in yours,
then shut inside
to free itself.

You have to wait
in the corner of the stone,
where the golden dust
of hope occasionally glints.

In the end the poem
will open itself. The stone
will let you out: a sheet of paper
that will begin to breathe.

David Huerta
'Nine Years Later – A Poem Dated'
Translated by Tom Boll and The Poetry Translation Centre Workshop

David Huerta was born in Mexico City in 1949. He has published nineteen books of poems and was included in *Medusario* (1996), the definitive anthology of neo-baroque Latin American poetry. His collections include *Cuaderno de noviembre* (1976), *Versión* (1978), from which 'Nine Years Later' is taken, and *Incurable* (1987), a verse-novel that brought him to the forefront of critical attention. In 2006 he was awarded the Xavier Villaurrutia prize for his lifelong contribution to Mexican literature. David Huerta will be giving a series of readings in the UK in spring 2010 as part of a tour organised by the Poetry Translation Centre.

Note on the translation process:

The workshops at the Poetry Translation Centre begin with a language expert presenting an original poem with a word for word crib of the literal sense. The group then attempts to create a translation that can function as a poem in English yet still retain the distinctive features of original text.

Nine Years Later – A Poem Dated

(The poem recalls the *Matanza de Tlatelolco* of 2 October 1968 when the Mexican military opened fire on students staging an anti-government protest in the Plaza de las Tres Culturas, Mexico City.)

I appeared in bloodstained October, my hands heavy with
    silence
and my eyes lashed to the dark.

If I spoke, my voice felt dislodged,
my bones were drenched with cold,
my legs, fluent with time, were carrying me out of the square
in a direction with no direction: to rebirth
in a hall of mirrors, the maze of streets.

The city razed by silence
was cut like quartz, slashes of slanting light portioned
the corners, the speechless bodies crushed against their lives,
but other bodies were there, there were other bodies.

I speak with my entire blood and from my own memories.
    And I am alive.

I ask myself, how are our eyes, our hands, our bones and our
    brain
after I left the square? Everything is solid, spacious and in
    flux,
after I left the square.

The air was telling me everything is still, is waiting.

I moved out of the square, my mouth scorched with
    memories,
and my blood fresh, shining like a ring continuously
coursing through my body, fully alive. So I was moving
out of the square, intact and breathing.

I breathed in images, and since then all those images come to
    me in dreams,
shattering everything, like wild horses.

Amid the turmoil of the day stood the mirror of death.
And a word from my life clung to an infinite edge.

I do not wish to speak of the scale of that afternoon,
nor place here adverbs, shouts or laments.

But I would like, yes, a flash of anger
to mark the mirror of death.
Where could I place my life, my words,
nine years later, but in that cold fury,
in that animal of rage that stirs, enamelling my dreams,
with its cruel breath?

All my blood circulates through my life, complete, without
    question.
But then I heard how it halted, bound to my breathing,
and beating, with the deaf call of its stillness, beating
my inner voices, the gestures of my human life,
the love I have been able to give and the death I will pass on.

Then fear came to my eyes to cover them with its frozen
    fingers.

All the silence of my body opened its alveoli
in front of the bodies laid waste, spat towards death by the
    zealous shrapnel:
those glistening bodies, bloody, silhouetted against the
    shredded light of late afternoon,
other bodies unlike mine, and even more different,
because they were uprooted, cleaved from human life
by a vertiginous fury, by the hands of a grievous force that
    cast itself, howling,
against those bodies, already fainter than the dusk,
yet more and more vivid in my waking dreams.

It is true I heard the shrapnel and now I write this,
it is true my blood now flows again and still I dream
with a kind of dead doubt, and sometimes I see my body
    naked
like a slow food for the devouring mouth of love.

Where were the bonds of my life,
my mirrors and my days, when afternoon fell on the square?

If I take a piece, a thread of my body and place it against the
    memory of that afternoon in the square,
I retreat to my life, frightened, as though the feather-light
    fingers of ghosts struck me in the mouth.

I speak about these weighty memories because I had to do it
    sometime, this way or another.

I left the square, a living stupor in my mouth and my eyes,
yet I felt my spit and my blood, still living.
It was a cool night, surrendered to time.
But in the streets, on the corners, in the bedrooms,
there were bodies, crushed and shut off from their lives by
    bitter fear.
A ring of fear was closing in on the city,
like a strange dream without end, without waking.

It was the mirror of death.
But death itself had already passed over with its armour and
    its instruments
into every corner, through all the cancelled air of the square.
It was the mirror of death with its reflections of fear
that brought shade to a city that was this city.

And in the street you could see how a hand was closing,
how an eye was blinking, how feet slid, in thick silence,
looking for an escape,
but there was no escape: only
a huge door open onto the kingdoms of fear.

October, 1977

Poets and Translators at the launch of *Frontiers* (Series 3, Number 11) at The Medical Foundation for the Care of Victims of Torture, 4th June 2009.

photos by Amarjit Chandan

Stephen Watts

Aviva Dautch

Hubert Moore

Nasrin Parvaz

Robert Hull

Robert Hull
At the Medical Foundation for the Care of Victims of Torture

A stream runs through the garden
in quiet sunlight.

Months, years, upstream from here,
or weeks or days

the hinterlands of dark –

their unimaginable cells –
their screaming corridors

their floors
running with
unutterable agony.

Hard to believe that now

a stream runs through a garden
in quiet sunlight

like a recovered voice.

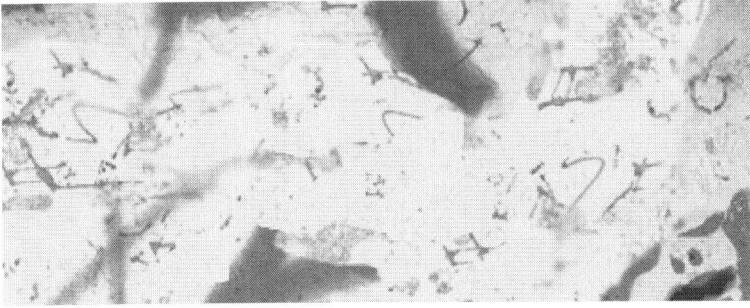

Bertolt Brecht
Ten poems
Translated by David Constantine

As in *MPT* 3/11, these are poems which are not readily, or at all, available in English. They are not in *Poems 1913–1956* nor in *Poems and Songs from the Plays* (Methuen 1976 and 1990, neither, at present, in print). All ten poems here are from 1920–21. In 1920 Brecht, aged twenty-two, moved from his home town Augsburg to Munich; spent time also in Berlin. His mother died, he was writing or rewriting *Baal, Drums in the Night,* many poems, seeking advancement in the literary world and 'enjoying' a complicated love life. The times were violent and pressing but only one of these ten poems, 'Political Observations', directly addresses them, and that in sardonic tones and very disengaged.

The poems are arranged chronologically and their location in the *Grosse kommentierte Berliner und Frankfurter Ausgabe* is given by volume and page, thus: 13,159

Ballad in the Hour of Despondency

1

I've had all the years I'll get.
Learned nothing, I'm an idiot.
Time to die, got no religion.
Brother, give me a drink or help me begone.

2

Wash your own face if your hands are mucky.
Mould and lime will cover it if you're lucky.
All things get used up and worn out down here
But my poxed scabby soul, where can I hide her?

3

Anyone seeing me in my shroud, please
I ask you now, comb my hair down over my eyes.
Cross yourself by all means but if you go white at the sight of
    me
So you would at the sight of any brute beast very likely.

13/159
This and the following three poems were written in the early part of
1920.

The river sings praises . . .

The river sings praises. Stars in the trees.
The smell of thyme and peppermint.
Our brows are freshened by a little breeze.
We are the children, this is God's present.
The grass is soft: the woman without bitterness.
The lovely willows make everything rejoice:
Pleasure's a certainty for those who will say yes.
Never again would you want to leave this place.

13/163
*Written 27 April 1920 for Paula Banholzer. Their son Frank was
born in 1919.*

My Brother's Death

Flung out in drink on the cold stones
Shaking, my brother raised his head to speak
And said he wanted no weeping, no one's
And gathered himself up in a last look.

He couldn't see us. Brightness blinded him.
He said nothing. His throat was tight.
His hand felt over his chest to find in him
A *heart* and then he told us straight:

Go away and shame on you. And all was very still.
These stones, he said, they are what's mine.
And let nobody weep. That is my will.
And none of us dared bother him again.

We stood aside.
He lay there drunk and mumbling till noon
And died then stealthily and fell apart at speed
Doubtless because he thought he wasn't seen.

13/163

The Prodigal Son

The pallid bushes in the mauve of Heaven
Often at nights they're like a sister's kiss to me
Towards midnight clouds drift over the face of Heaven
Very white and very lovably.

To beautiful women I was a cause of sorrow
When I'd eaten my fill and they left me they were sad
The nights have been very warm for some time now
Only towards morning is the grass a chilly bed.

And if one night, being tired, I fall through Heaven's door
At least there's someone knows about my Fall
Cold waking early I feel my throat. They were
Only the hands of nightmare after all.

Mild Heaven and the winds so blue and good
Are well disposed to me on my way down

I sleep at nights the way I slept in childhood
In many waters I've washed myself clean.

And when I've blisters on my feet, why then
Peppermint cools them as a sister might
And while I sleep my wild hair tangles in
The bitter-smelling lilies through the night.

Heaven is big. One bad dog going about
In a big field's really no concern of his
He's not small-minded, he bestows his light
On the whole wide world and everything that is.

13/164

Again and again there were red evenings . . .

1
Again and again there were red evenings
The smell of asphalt and the smell of thyme
They lived always expecting He would kill them
But He was lax and that was not His game.

2
The heavens radiant like the enormous lies
Made fools of them. It held them up, all that.
He wished to know just how long they could bear it
But they were clueless and never thought of that.

3

And when they asked was it His wish that they
Renounce, then too He did not speak
And left them standing in a dark wood
Without a word and veiled Himself in smoke.

4

But they said yes into the uncertainty
Gave up and fell upon their knees. That way
Quite soon their bitternesses ceased to be
(And somewhat sooner so did they.)

13/175
Written mid-1920.

Political Observations

For hours they row around on the town lake
It disgusts me to watch them. For heaven's sake
Rowing around on a pond and we're up to our ears in debt
The mess the country's in, I'm surprised they allow it

I hang around smoking and watching, that's what I do
And I think my thoughts, that's pretty much what I do
Another thing in this place, they play the mouth organ.
The land's in the grip of the Black Plague and they play the
    mouth organ

And I think coldly, carry on playing, carry on rowing up and
    down
And I spit, but really beyond that it's no concern of mine
I've hung around watching for some years now
And I see exactly where we are rowing to

I read in *From Pole to Pole* that the inhabitants of Orkney
Did each other's washing for a living. Well okay
Carry on a few more years like this, just you carry on
They were great ones for boating in Assyria too and in
    Babylon

13/194
*Written around 1920. 'The Black Plague' (in German 'die schwarze
Schande') may be a direct allusion to a medal issued in 1920 by the
Munich artist Karl Goetz, the two faces of which amount to a racist
polemic against the presence of black French soldiers in the occupied
Rhineland.* From Pole to Pole *was a popular travel book. (Robert
Graves, in the Foreword to his* Poems 1938–45, *relates the same story
about the Scilly Islanders.) Brecht himself is much closer to the rowers
and the harmonica-players than to the speaker of this poem.*

Balaam Lai in his thirtieth year . . .

Balaam Lai in his thirtieth year
Sailed one evening for Madagascar
Because of a longing to see Erna Susatte
Because it was four years since he'd
Seen her
And where she was he had no idea
And so he thought: She's in Madagascar.

He looked at the map in Thomas Cook's. She'd
Very likely be there somewhere
He thought and so
He landed up in Madagascar
Rather
As Pontius Pilate did in the Creed.

He travelled with a case full of documents
An umbrella badly in need of splints
A guitar and a bottle of Johnny Walker
And trouble in the heart, an old disorder.
But the sea is a damned bad-mannered critter
So he didn't give much thought to Erna Susatte
But once he was on the island then
The name (not the face) occurred to him again
But that night he went to bed alone, supposing
He'd hardly come across her the very first evening.

So when Balaam Lai in his thirtieth year
Suddenly one morning was in Madagascar
He asked himself before he went in search of her
Whether it was possible Erna Susatte
Was in Madagascar
And concluding it was possible, why shouldn't it be?
But that his chances of finding her were slight, especially
Since all he'd got with him was a suitcase and an umbrella
And since moreover the interest that he
Still had in the face of the vanished Erna Susatte
Was not great, not very great
And deciding over a vilely concocted punch
That Madagascar wasn't up to much
He sailed home moderately drunk on punch but
Shot of all the yearning and longing muck
And ordered another punch at The Red Carnation
12 Tauenziehenstrasse, run
By another Erna, surnamed Clouds, this one.

Many years later, same street, number 4, in a bar
A supersaturated drunk used to relate
Among various true stories this one about
A daring trip in a schooner to Madagascar
Shipwreck, visions, snakebites
And a face he had seen deep in the swamps of Madagascar
As proof that now and then miracles do happen
For example when
With nothing to go on
He sees the pale and forgotten face of Erna Susatte
In an Asiatic
Swamp, drunk as a skunk on punch.

13/212
Written 1921.
*In this and the final poem Brecht adopts a strange persona and views
his love life with bleak amusement in an exotic imagery. Pontius
Pilate got into the Creed 'accidentally'. Tauenzienstrasse is a street
in Berlin. 'Clouds' (German: 'Gewölk'), used as a surname for Erna
or, in other poems, Anna, suggests that love, the beloved, the lover are
more fleeting even than clouds are. See the next poem and also especially
'Erinnerung an die Marie A.' (Remembering Marie A.), written
February 1920.*

Now in the night . . .

1
Now in the night while I love you
White clouds are in the silence in the sky
The waters make a roaring over stones
And the wind shivers in dead greenery.

2
White waters hurry
Down year after year
And in the sky there are
Clouds for evermore.

3
Later in the years of loneliness
Still there will be white clouds to see
And the waters will make a roaring over stones
And the wind will shiver in dead greenery.

13/216
Written 1921

There at the beginning . . .

There at the beginning, the first day
When that entwining couple entered here
The threshold knew they would not get away
It took the footfall that would be their last.
Behind the lattice the green tree sank to sere
And yellow discreetly, very fast
And climbing trembling to bed they were
With a smile by the wind they loved dismissed.

13/217
Written 1921.

Balaam Lai in July

In July after the decline and fall of the Marquise
And his expulsion from Paradise
Standing in the dead bulrushes
At a pond with flies
Buzz buzz
Balaam Lai, supersaturated drunk that he was
Balaam Lai got smitten by the sun
God help us!
Balaam Lai, spirituous spirit of The White Carnation
Spat offhandedly into the pond of flies
Splash
Chewed things over and composed an invitation
To Anna Clouds
To join him that night in a solemn lamentation
And went and purchased another pair of duck eggs.
God have mercy on Anna Clouds!

But when the evening palely and in great pain began to
    darken
Balaam Lai had doubts
When Anna Clouds in the twilight came
Sailing along with her parasol, white as cream.
For Anna Clouds when it came to it was quite without
Any false delicacy in her free views
On love, God knows, she was the last person
To be fobbed off with lousy conjuring tricks
And not judge a man on his performance as though
He fed on the wafers of the Lord and raw eggs
And Balaam Lai knew this.
In brief, she observed that windows are made of glass
And when he didn't draw the curtains she did
And at eight o' clock was lounging on Balaam Lai's lily-pad
(Whilst he like grim death read the *Evening News*).

Now when Anna Clouds began chewing her pink toes for
    boredom
Balaam Lai gave rapid thought as to how
This unchaste creature could be evicted from his wigwam
But saw no way and the best he could do
He thought, was trot off and buy red wine and quickly get
Her very drunk on it.

And she might pass out
While he sat over a noble and corpulent tome oppressed
By the decline and fall of the West.
But she, full of wine and wriggling around on his cushions,
Stared him stiff to share
What had occurred to her.
In brief, she slugged the bottles and was the cold-soberest
Most frivolous person on earth when with all the winningness
Of a valkyrie desperate for corpses
She invited him to join her in a little tenderness.

13/231
Written 1921
Losing the Marquise, Balaam Lai ill-advisedly turns to the
redoubtable Anna Clouds. The 'noble and corpulent tome' sounds
like Oswald Spengler's Decline of the West. *In Germanic myth the*
Valkyries hovered over the battlefield and fetched the dead to Valhalla.

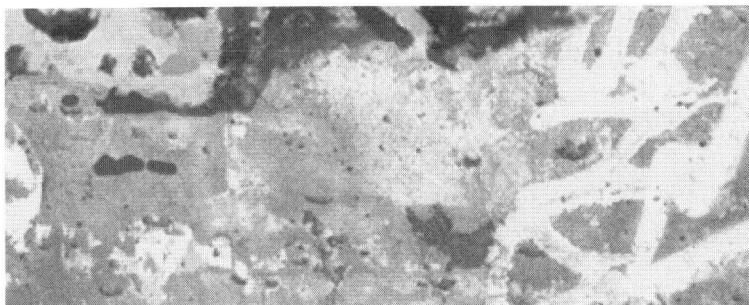

Michael Foley
'Wang Wei in Exile'

Having parents unhappy with their status and each other,
  disappointed, cold,
And coarse friends who loathed books but loved pelting stray
  cats with stones,
I read time and again the tale of Peach Blossom Spring and
  the fisherman
Who followed the blossoming trees to the stream and cave
Which grew low and narrow but opened out suddenly into
  another world
Where people dressed and looked the same but were
  magnanimous and blithe.
Then I'd read T'ao Ch'ien's poem on the story and repeat the
  last line:
I long to rise and ride the wind in search of my own kind.
No more unfulfilled yearning. I would seek out my people –
  follow the spring,
Find the magical aperture and pass beyond – the secret
  sustaining dream
That made me remote, often obstinate, loath to participate,
Despising the peevishness, observing the rituals with a
  contemptuous smirk.

Oh no such spring of course – but there would happen
  something marvellous.
A summons would come – and I would be ready, having read
  and pondered deeply
To make my imagination strong. For whatever came would
  not be mundane.
An ardour and expectation that lasted for decades but died in
  this barbarous town
In the west that believes itself the centre of the universe and
  endowed
With exemplary forthrightness (insults), intelligence (guile)
  and generosity (bribes).
Even the mildest reciprocal candour would needless to say
  cause an outcry.
They demand that the government official work for them,
Then despise him for a fool when he does. The sort of clever
  diligent fool
Who gets first place in examinations but can't do the
  simplest deal.
This much the same as at court – detachment's what they
  sense and hate.
Forgotten in the capital and disregarded here, daily I grow
Insubstantial, uncertain, a prey to hallucination, anxiety and
  foreboding.
I shave . . . my father's face in the mirror (at last with a tiny
  smile,
Albeit rueful). Then it's blank. I'm the ghost – and the very
  mirror
Seems to look past . . . or through . . . out beyond at ragged
  clouds and grey sky,
Another of those desultory days that become the years and
  your only life.

Note

Wang Wei is famous as a visual poet with a Buddhist affinity for nature. But what makes him more interesting than many such poets is an unresolved tension between this mysticism and a worldly interest in the pleasures of capital and court. Like many of us he had to work to pay for wine to sip while contemplating the white clouds and he frequently found his official duties demeaning, never more so than during his exile from court, where he was Assistant Secretary for Music, to a minor post in Shantung province. He learned from this experience and on his return to the capital after a few years astutely maintained a career as a 'half-recluse', even managing to survive the overthrow of the government by rebel forces. So he is an inspiration to all those who gaze from office desks at a patch of sky. Pound described him as a 'Jules Laforgue chinois', 'the real modern – even Parisian – of VIII cent. China'.

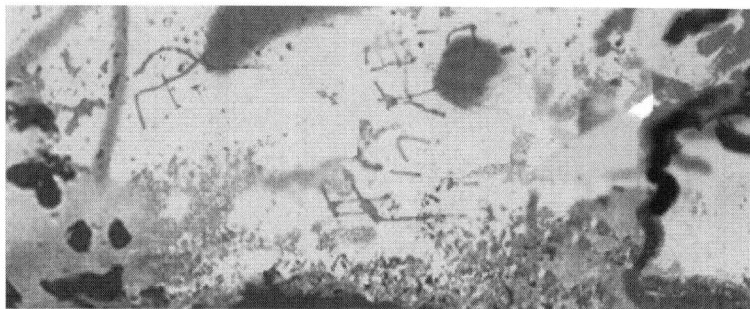

Wang Wei
'Autumnal Dusk in the Mountains'
Translated by Julian Farmer

The poetry of Wang Wei (699–761 AD) is somewhat plain and austere but is filled with visual and spiritual insights. He is a Chinese poet of the Tang period, which is surely the most highly regarded.

He was born into a prosperous family, his father being a local official and his mother coming from a family with literary pedigree. In his mid teens, Wang Wei went to the capital and soon gained favour on account of his exceptional talent. But he found himself removed to the provinces again and bought himself his famous country estate on the Wang River, where he cultivated his love of simplicity and nature.

Principally, he was a devout Buddhist. Not only did he flourish as a poet, but he was also valued as a painter. Despite the fact that none of his originals survive, there is a whole school of Chinese painting descended from his work. He was an accomplished musician. His 'Three Variations on the Yang Pass', a setting of a poem about exile, is still played. Wang Wei worked all his life in administrative posts and cunningly survived being forced to work in a rebel government. He became a widower in his early thirties, was childless, and never remarried.

山居秋暝

空山新雨后，
天气晚来秋。
明月松间照，
请泉石上流。
竹喧归浣女，
莲动下渔舟。
随意春芳歇，
王孙自可留。

王维

Autumnal Dusk in the Mountains

On the bare mountain, rain has just passed.
The weather is gloomy. Autumn is on its way.
The bright moon shines between the pines.
A clear spring trickles over a rock.
Bamboos rustle. A woman returns from washing.
Lotuses stir beneath a fishing boat.
I long for the coming spring and rest.
The world and his wife can come and stay.

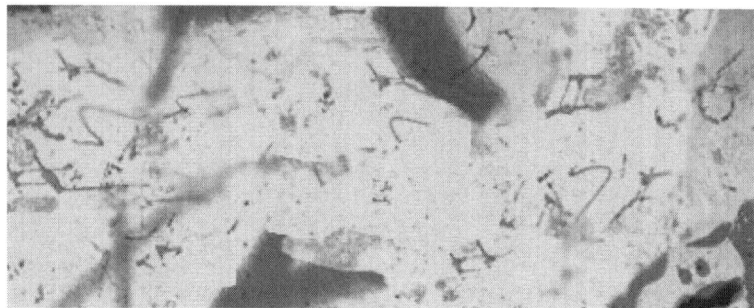

Jennie Feldman
Olive Trees, West Bank

As for you, my captive
olive tree,
a splendid evening to you,
my tree of enduring captivity,
branches of the everlasting journey . . .

(From 'The Evening Wine of Aged Sorrow')*

At a recent event in East Jerusalem in his honour, the acclaimed Palestinian Israeli poet Taha Muhammad Ali was reading from a new bilingual volume of his work, and once again I was struck by his own likeness to the venerable olive tree – the profoundly lined face crowned with silvery glints in the lamplight, the age-old rooted resilience against the odds. Indeed since that evening the theme of the olive has, like the poetry, persisted in my thoughts.

*Taha Muhammad Ali, *So What: New and Selected Poems 1971-2005*, trans. Peter Cole, Yahya Hijazi, Gabriel Levin (Copper Canyon Press, 2006). The same evening, Adina Hoffman presented her new biography of Taha Muhammad Ali, *My Happiness Bears No Relation to Happiness: A Poet's Life in the Palestinian Century* (Yale University Press, 2009).

In this region, where virtually everything – animal, vegetable, mineral – is charged with political significance, the ubiquitous olive tree has a mute eloquence all its own. On the road from Jerusalem to Bethlehem, where the tall grey slabs of the Separation Wall suddenly block your way and wind off into the low hills, the rows of olive trees – which continue unseen on the other side – greet me soberly every Sunday morning, leaves trembling slightly. Together we wait for two young Palestinian boys, Yakub and Majid, to come through the checkpoint with their mothers for their regular dialysis treatment in a West Jerusalem hospital. Unsurprisingly, the NGO that brought us together began as The Olive Tree Movement *before it became* Humans Without Borders.***

Because olives are vital to the Palestinian economy, and the olive groves on the West Bank constitute a visible, vulnerable expression of land ownership, they have long been the target of sabotage by Jewish settlers. In response, anti-Occupation human rights groups and peace organizations in Israel have developed programmes of practical help for Palestinian olive farmers. Last time I went with other volunteers for a day's olive-picking across the Green Line, I brought back these impressions.

On a chill Thursday morning, Abu Rami is at the wheel as we leave Jerusalem, pass the checkpoints and head north into the West Bank. A seasoned activist with Israel's left-wing Peace Now movement, he's fielding calls to his mobile from both sides of the Green Line, switching between Arabic and Hebrew as reflexively as he changes gears. Our minibus speeds through the hills on route 60 under a dawn slung with low clouds. 'It's not going to rain, is it?' he asks. 'Not according to the forecast,' someone assures him. His passengers are eight volunteers on their way to join Palestinian farmers for the all-important olive harvest; this, like other agricultural activity, has been severely hampered

**Humans Without Borders is an Israeli non-profit organization whose activities include arranging for volunteers to take chronically ill West Bank Palestinians, often children, from the checkpoints to their hospital appointments in Israel.

by settler violence, army restrictions and/or the Separation
Wall. Another few weeks and the olive-picking season will be
over.

A coordinated network of such sorties into the West Bank
has been in operation for several years now, taking a message
of solidarity to Palestinians under Israeli occupation. Prominent
among the various groups involved is Rabbis for Human Rights
(RHR), a widely respected organization which calls itself 'the
rabbinic voice of conscience in Israel' and has received several
awards. Today's trip is part of its year-round activities. Arik –
RHR executive director, rabbi Arik Ascherman – has already
briefed us on essentials: avoid confrontation, stay calm, protect
the Palestinian farmers, take photos that can be used as evidence.
The day's plan has been coordinated with the Israel Defence
Forces. We are given information sheets with contact numbers
for RHR, the Israel police, the IDF, and each other, in case we
get separated.

My fellow travellers are all Israelis. Beside me are a computer
programmer and a librarian, both semi-retired, both old hands
at the business of demonstrations and confrontations. One breaks
off from an account of an anti-Wall rally to point to a garage
we've just passed (by now we are a few miles south of Nablus):
'See that place? A few weeks ago an Israeli took his car there to
have it fixed – because of the cheaper prices – and they killed
him.' The other shakes his head slowly, 'Probably thought he was
a settler.'

Newly greened by the first rains, the hills sweep by in an age-
old rhythm of terraced olive groves and sinuous valleys. We're not
far from biblical Shiloh, where the daughters of the city danced
in the vineyards and were seized by the Benjaminites. Curiosity
has had me flipping through Judges to that last chapter. Its final
sentence carried a shock of recognition: 'In those days there was
no king in Israel; everyone did as he pleased.' All who heard or
read the speech by Israeli writer David Grossman at the memorial
gathering for Yitzhak Rabin a few years ago will remember his
stinging indictment then, which time has only confirmed: *Ein*

melekh be'israel – 'There is no king in Israel . . . our leadership is hollow . . .'

Today we're being assigned to three Palestinian villages on the West Bank that have asked RHR for help in the face of settler aggression. I and Maya, a woman in her mid-fifties, are dropped off at Karyut, population about 3,000, where we're joined by two young female volunteers, from the US and Sweden. Outside the community centre, its metal gate daubed with a huge Palestinian flag, a member of the village council beams a welcome and we head off on foot down the hill and across the valley, rich red earth clinging to every tread as we sidestep mauve patches of autumn crocus.

(A sudden flashback to a similar scene a few years ago, not far from here. We were a Saturday busload from Haifa, organized by Ta'ayush – the Arabic name means 'living together', 'life in common' – an Israeli association set up by Jewish and Palestinian activists during the early stages of the second Intifada. Most of the group had already been dropped off at the designated villages; the remainder, about fifteen of us, were waiting beside the bus to be ferried by the villagers to outlying olive groves in a scrambled assortment of cars and vans. Then an IDF patrol came by and there ensued a lengthy debate between the officer and our coordinator. Precious time was passing; our frustration mounted. At one point the two men moved a little way off, presumably for discretion's sake. That was our cue to dive into the waiting vehicles. A surreal moment as we sped off down the dirt track – Palestinians and Israelis crammed together, chortling at the small shared victory.)

A few of the stone houses of Karyut balance on the skyline behind us as we finally reach the terraces where Salomon and Aziz, wiry and grey-stubbled, are already hard at work. 'Buonas díaz!' comes the unexpected greeting from Salomon, who brought back from his years in South America an exuberant fluency in Spanish. They're picking on the lower terraces; the upper ones, abutting the new settlement of Shvut Rachel, are too risky to approach unaccompanied, as attacks by settlers are commonplace.

This is the first year the council of Karyut has approached RHR for help. A couple of weeks ago the villagers had made an early start on their own and rocks were hurled at them. One man had to be hospitalized.

We climb to the topmost terrace, where only a patrol road and a fence separate us from the new houses on the crest, their hallmark red-tiled roofs visible for miles. Here the olive trees, untended for four years, have a wild, unkempt look. We set to, 'milking' the branches and letting the purplish olives patter onto the sacking cloth spread below. It's not long before an army jeep approaches. Polite greetings are exchanged. Has there been any trouble? we are asked. No, all quiet. They stay on anyway, evidently assigned to keep an eye on things. Some time later, the settlers' security patrol draws up near the jeep and a young man comes half-running towards us, waving his arms and shouting in Hebrew: 'Thieves! Thieves! Clear off! This is disputed land!' We point out that the IDF – the patrol is still there – has raised no objection to our picking, and resume work. The man eventually stalks off, muttering threats. We are all aware that had the two villagers been alone, the outcome would have been very different.

We're making good progress, when two soldiers from the jeep walk over and quietly say they've received orders from their commander not to allow any work on these upper terraces – the 'disputed land' – next to the settlement, since such activity could serve as cover for a terror attack. But look, we reason, today we are four women and two old men – not a likely threat. All the same, they insist, just move down four terraces, out of sight of the settlement. How about two terraces, we counter – bargaining being a way of life in these parts – so as not to skip so many trees?

The picking activity begins to shift downhill, not without protest. At one point the Swedish student, a steely beauty straight out of Nordic mythology, goes over to the two soldiers. Out of earshot, their exchange has a potent visual eloquence: confronted by this indignant goddess, the two young conscripts appear to say less and less, as if they've briefly forgotten their lines, musing instead on the lost joys of normalcy.

In bursts of sun between the clouds, the waiting olives glow dark and plump as grapes. Most can be reached from the ground, but we climb up for the topmost. When we're tempted to go after every last one before relinquishing a tree, Aziz and Salomon keep the pace brisk – *Khalas*! Enough! Move on! Whatever their inward pain and bitterness over The Situation, they keep a laconic good humour. It seems that over the years, disillusion has learned to comport itself graciously, even as it sharpens the wits. 'A peasant . . . / the son of a peasant,' writes Palestinian Israeli poet Taha Muhammad Ali, 'there lies within me / a mother's sincerity / and a fishmonger's guile.'

Salomon's genial son Ahmed, an unemployed graphic designer, arrives with a tractor, a donkey and lunch: humous, pitta, falafel and 7-Up, which he dishes out with a flourish. Talk revolves around matters of food and family, with English the lingua franca, but only just. One senses, though, that even if we visitors were fluent in Arabic, deep-seated political views – beyond reports on this or that incident – would not be discussed with us. In any case, no fluency could adequately convey one's sense of outrage and injustice at what is happening here, so it's something of a relief to let actions speak instead.

Eventually the three men call a halt for the day. The sacks of olives are hoisted onto the ledge behind the tractor, Salomon sets off astride the donkey, Aziz starts the engine, and we four women perch on the wheel rims. Back in Karyut, passing villagers hail us in Arabic-inflected English and – surprisingly – Hebrew. Ahmed invites us into his spacious new house. Sitting on cushions we sip cinnamon tea served by his wife, and admire his cherubic daughter.

Dusk has already dimmed the contours of the West Bank as Arik's car heads back to Jerusalem. Long before we reach the army barrier where the road cuts through the looming Wall, updates on the day's activities start coming in on the car phone. 'We're still on the hill,' one woman is saying. 'Their donkey's lame so it's a slow business getting the olives to the road. . . . There's trouble. . . . I'm trying not to get arrested. . . .' The accounts are unrelievedly grim: pickers turned back, closure orders, stones and threats from settlers. We learn that the Karyut council member who had taken us out to the groves had been warned, after escorting other volunteers to a different site, that if the settlers saw him there again they would kill him. Guard dogs have been tied to olive trees as a deterrent, a grove has been set ablaze. . . . Appalled silence now as Arik drives on. 'Things seem to be getting worse,' someone comments. 'Yes,' comes the matter-of-fact response. Settlers have stepped up their violence in reaction to the government decision to dismantle 'illegal outposts'. On the other hand, he points out, there is a High Court ruling in place – following a petition submitted by RHR in 2004 – that the army is responsible for protecting Palestinian farmers and their property during the olive harvest. (Arrested on more than one occasion for trying to block house demolitions in East Jerusalem, Arik has a first-hand acquaintance with the legal process.) He keeps a copy of the ruling in his pocket for those instances when army personnel need reminding. The car phone rings again: for next week's ploughing in the south Hebron hills, says the caller, will *rav Arik* please send volunteers . . . just to be there in case of trouble. . . .

Coda

whose Wall is it anyway?
mine says the quail
pinned to its shadow

mine says the boy slotted
by halves through a gap
to sell trinkets

yours says the grey
stilted thing stalking
what small hope

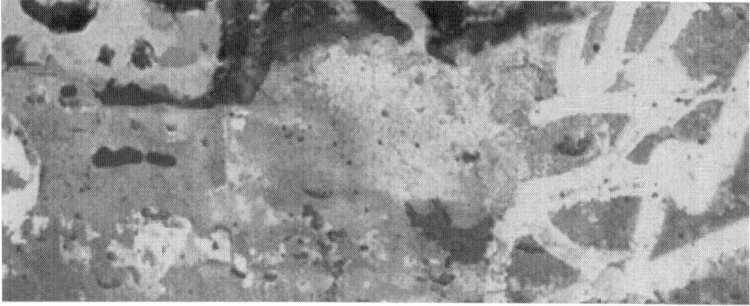

Chris Beckett
Six Ethiopian Poems

I grew up in Ethiopia and am trying to explore the nature of an Ethiopian boyhood, with the help of some traditional verse forms, such as praise shouts (for an important person or horse or car, even a day of the week), laments and boasts (self-praises).

Ethiopia has more than seventy ethnic groups and languages, so as many poetic traditions. I am not an expert on any of them, I just imitate poems which I have read or heard, and liked. A lot of this poetry is oral or sung, only recorded when an academic goes into the field to hear the unsanitised views of rural people on, for example, a terrible famine or jigger fleas or corrupt politicians. It is a poetry of protest and complaint, as well as praise, sometimes in the voice of the object of protest, the famine or the flea, for example, so a sort of ironic boast.

Poems take the form of a short pithy verse of 2/4 lines, full of puns and similes and internal/final rhymes. Sometimes the poem is just one verse, sometimes it piles verses and repetitions/refrains up into a much longer poem, moving forward by taking a word or image in one line and repeating it with a twist in the next.

Horse Song

(imitation of an ox lament from the Kafa highlands of Ethiopia)

O, my horse, let me sing!
O, my smoky horse, who neighed
   like a wind in the big rains
   like a drill at the new airport, let me sing!
my horse, who galloped out of rusty gates
whose tail was still in the stable while his head swept
   past the church of Yeka Mikael
O, my horse, let me sing!
O, my speedy horse, who overtook buses of every make
   lorded it over mules and pissed on dung-beetles
your mane was a flag
your legs were marathon runners
you were not for the gharry trot-trot or carty sticks to market
you weren't even for the lucky boy to enjoy riding
you were for the pride of being a horse
O, my horse, let me sing!
O, my fidgety horse, who liked to ripple the skin
   up/down your body, let me sing!
you threw flies off your carpet
you threw dust-writing up in the air, telling other horses
   where you'd gone
O, my horse, where have you gone?
O, my brotherly horse, who took me out of the backseat
   out of the stuffy windows
who rode you after I went away?
who saw the world from your back, felt your blood beating
   under his knees?
O, my horse, let me sing!
O, my sleek horse, what are these shabby bone-bundles
   clopping down Yeka Road?

Dirge for Mrs Ethiopia

*(in the voices of at least ten boys aged eight to twelve, sometimes singing
alone, sometimes in two's or three's and sometimes all together)*

Whose legs swell like a river?
whose ankles burst open like watermelons in the sun?

> *wai amlaki!*
> *wai-wai-wai!*

it is our Mother whose legs are ruined
our Mother, the always singing and laughing woman
her generous thighs slapped like a hundred drums
    when she pounded the t'ef
her smooth oily knees clicked like bicycle gears
    when she chased a chicken

> *wai amlaki!*
> *wai-wai-wai!*

Mother! we are the boys who visit, holding a daisy and an
    orange
and we are the sick boys, too, on our clanky beds and trolleys
    malaria boys!
    bilharzia boys!
even the little red-boy shivering to himself in a corner

> *wai amlaki!*
> *wai-wai-wai!*

but Mother! you were always laughing
even yesterday at five after the doctor's visit and the long
    injections and cinnamon tea
you were humming like a Friday afternoon girl
you were laughing like a Sunday morning lady
so our Ward Sister clacked her tongue, saying
araa! my auntie, why so giggle, when you are very sick?

> *wai amlaki!*
> *wai-wai-wai!*

look now! Mother, the sun is bright this morning
but our hearts are full of clouds
we are the dark boys beating our chests to clay
tying white cloths around our necks

> *wai amlaki!*
> *wai-wai-wai!*

wait! do not run off yet on your afterlife legs
we are pouring out of our classrooms and jumping
    out of our sick-beds
we are shaking the sleepy churches and hunting
    the wicked mosquito
we will clap and wail and question every teacher
    every politician
    every nurse and clerk

> *wai amlaki!*
> *wai-wai-wai!*

because we are struggling, Mother
who will carry us if you are lying down?
who will care for us
if the box of your traditional and modern medicines
    rattles like a pea?
who will laugh for us
when we have lost our sense of humour?

                    wai amlaki!
                    wai-wai-wai!

Notes:
wai amlaki: woe to God!
t'ef: fine grain used for making injera

Goat, Donkey and Dog

(in the style of Kebede Mikael)

Once upon a time, little friend,
Goat, Donkey and Dog
took a taxi to the Monday market.
Now how should they divide the fare?
With many *ba*'s and *haw*'s and *bark*'s
they finally agreed that
each of them would pay a third.
But Goat searched every fold of skin
and couldn't find a single birr,
so he butted at the door and ran away.
Then Donkey shook a smallish note
from the wallet of his right ear

and offered it politely clamped
in his long yellow teeth,
while Dog turned paw to palm
and handed over a twenty,
crisp as any Monday morning,
and waited on the kerb for change.

But the driver was that kind of man
who God tests by giving him a car,
and once behind the wheel
he loses sight of his humanity,
his eyes become narrow and greedy
because he believes that
no-one else has such a dashing taxi!
no-one else can go as fast as him!
He forgets to say to himself:
Yefat, you have the speed of lizards,
but you cannot make milk like a goat,
you cannot cart firewood like a donkey
or guard the house like a dog.
Yefat, you are still just a man
with two legs for walking into church
and two knees for praying!

So all the taxi driver did was laugh
and spit and speed away...
and that is why, little friend,
the Goat runs off whenever a car appears,
why Donkey always stands so stiff
and righteous in the middle of the road
and it is also why Dog, poor cheated Dog!
always barks at cars and chases them
and tries to bite their tyres.

Motorcar!

the one who roars at gates and donkeys
the one with more doors than a house
the one with two rich tones of skin colour and a swishy
    v-shaped tail
the one who takes neat heads to school
 who takes sorrow to the airport
the one with strange songs bubbling out of his window
    as he dusts off to market
the one who always holds his warm nose out of the mud
the one we like to tap and brother as he shoulders
    along our street
the one who gets a splashy sponge and rub-down every
    morning by his own boy
the one we own with our shiny eyes
the one called *Zephyr*, waxy and proud!

To the man with a guzzler wife

You who have a guzzler wife,
divorce her and wait for me.

My name is Dubbala, voice of famine!
I am a hot wind in the marketplace,
soon I will hammer on your flimsy door.

Here I am with wide-open eyes,
with my eyes that are burning.
You should look for a shrub to hide under.

I will suck the water from your rivers,
chew the beans on your coffee bushes,
brown the grass so your cows shrink to no-milk.

Don't boast that you're so-and-so's friend!
Don't big-talk that you're the son of Mr Rich.
I have seen you by the road with your begging bag.

The last injera is baked but brother swears to brother:
'I have not one inch of eating left!'
Yes! salvation of the soul is a thing of the past.

I am bad days coming and days that are worse than that.
I am the end of *here comes a donkey loaded with lentils,*
the start of *I swapped my mother for a taba of beans.*

I am the green algae choking your well-water!
I am the hand who gives your sister to the vultures!
The poor are beating me, the rich hurt my eyes.

Note:

The epigraph is from *Unheard Voices: Drought, Famine and God in Ethiopian Oral Poetry,* by Fekade Azeze (Addis Ababa University Press, 1998). My poem is a collage of lines freely adapted from the 2- or 3-line poems collected in Professor Azeze's book. It is meant as a sample of and a homage to the amazing poems in that book.

Poem to Friday

(after a festive Oromo song)

O Friday! be friendly
you rain on our tin roof
you wet-shoe my Pap
and hair-soak my Mam

O Friday! be friendly
it's end-of-week dinner
weekly fry-day for fish
weekly cuddle for Mam

O Friday! be friendly
tell the nile-perch, be crispy
tell the peppers, be prickly
soak our bread in rich sauce

O Friday! be friendly
Mam's dropping her frypan
Pap's ouching and hopping
my brothers are scrapping

O Friday! be friendly
shrink the egg on Pap's big toe
throw salt on my brothers
jump our fish off the floor

O Friday! be friendly
don't dark while we're eating
don't flood through a window
keep our happiness dry!

Note:

The Oromo song is much longer and full of elephants! They are part of the landscape, of course, but they're mainly there because of the pun on *arbi* (Friday) versus *arba* (elephant), both of which also assonate with *arari* (propitious). I have tried using *Friday* and *friendly* to recreate this sort of effect, but alas without elephants!

Patrice de La Tour du Pin
'Children of September'
Translated by Padraig Rooney

Patrice de La Tour du Pin (1911–1975) spent his childhood in the Gatinais region of central France, a psycho-geography which has infiltrated much of his poetry. His father was killed at the Battle of the Marne. Brought up by his mother, the great grand-daughter of the Irish parliamentarian General Arthur O' Connor, La Tour du Pin published 'Les Enfants de Septembre' in *La Nouvelle Revue Française* when he was just nineteen. *La Quête de joie* (1933) established his reputation. Imprisoned in Germany during the Second World War, he evolved a mystical-religious cycle, Catholic, noble and Celtic in tone, stretching over fifty years, and published definitively as *Somme de poésie* (1981).

Children of September

The sodden woods were quiet underfoot
and blanketed in ground fog, deserted.
A north wind brought them down among us
at dusk – September children winging in
on spaceships, UFOs high in the sky.

At night I felt the brush of wings descend
in search of hideouts, crevices where children
like them while away the day recuperating
and licking wounds. Their inconsolable cry
echoes off the bird-deserted marshland.

At dawn I left the squalor of my room
and headed for the woods, along a path
beneath an amber moon that rode the fog.
I caught their feral trace, the spoor of game
on moonlit tracks – a wild September child

whose scuffled footprints seemed to dance at first
along the ruts and then were lost in bog.
Surreptitiously, he quenched his thirst
and dallied there at games of make-believe
in rain-soaked undergrowth, as night came on.

I lost his tracks beneath a stand of beech
where, hardly touching ground, they petered out.
I stalked him, thought he'd double back at dawn
to reconnoitre with his flight companions,
on tenterhooks in case they'd upped and gone.

How sure I was he would return to haunt
these moonlit bridle paths and eerie clearings
where bucks interrogate the morning breeze
suspiciously before they break for cover
and skeins of geese head south in stark formation

across the frozen bog where day was breaking.
I made myself a blind, a camouflage
and hunkered down to watch nocturnal fauna
emerge to drink their fill from standing pools
beneath a parliament of raucous crows.

September's child, I knew, was me incarnate,
my spitting image, a game *enfant sauvage*
with feverish limbs and fervour in his loins.
What sends me out along the roads at night
in search of him is fire in the blood.

September's child will surely take me in
beneath his wing and treat me like a brother.
My mesmerising eyes will cast their spell
unless I take him by surprise and run
across the forest floor to pinion him.

Then, like a wounded bird, he'll bat his wings
at my approach. I'll track him down until
the fight, the flight, goes out of him, defeated.
His wild-child wings will beat no more and fold,
his downcast eyes resigned to certain death.

And then I'll lay him sleeping in my arms,
and stroke the feathers on his worn-out wings
and carry home his tiny gosling warmth
across the rushy marshland where in time
he'll wake to find me smiling down at him.

Again the line of fog through winter trees,
the gusts of northern wind that penetrate
your shriven bones and leave them blown apart
like all who ventured on this path before you,
who flew against prevailing winds and lost.

And so September's children won't descend
or bother with this washed-out hinterland
deprived of legend, tonight or any night.
Not one among them has the spunk to stray
or comprehend this god-forsaken bog.

Ivan Teofilov
Six poems
Translated by Jonathan Dunne

Ivan Teofilov, born in Bulgaria's second largest city, Plovdiv, in 1931, is a playwright and poet. A graduate of Sofia's National Academy of Theatre and Film Arts, he worked as a playwright in Burgas and Ruse and as a director for the National Puppet Theatre. He was chief editor of the *Popular Library of Contemporary World Poetry* series created by Narodna Kultura, poetry editor for *Plamak* magazine and founding editor of the magazine *Sezon*. He has published nine poetry collections, the last two being *Geometry of the Spirit* (which won the National Poetry Award in 1996) and *Infinitive* (which won the National Literature Award in 2004). His other books include plays, an *Anthology of Bulgarian Symbolism* and *Monologues*, a collection of travel essays.

In Nature

The falcon. Its symmetrical confession –
in circles of light and vertigo.

Wedding ring of the wind.

Gruff hymn
of the air and rock.

Up above.

Down below –
in the intervals of spacious life –
hardly anyone will learn about the breath
of the ant and clover,
which are one and the same confession,
and illumined thought, and trembling pain,
and sultry circles of love . . .

. . . under sun slides and echoes
of the Infinite, which is
another memory of theirs. And soul.

Chair

Left by chance in the middle of the garden,
its face towards the mountain, growing light
in the netted quivering shadows.

And I after such a long time
saw in the chair the line of a seated man.

And I after such a long time
thought of man, who invented
the candour of the seated form.

(Now that I appreciate life better,
missed values hit me
more and more . . .)

The Fruit Bowl

Sun floods the room, which
bulges with tender objectivity:
pictures, cupboards, armchairs yell
with ever more insistent knowledge
of their living presence.
And suddenly like a cry of light
next to the shelf-ticking alarm clock
a simple product goes into ecstasy –
the old, repulsive fruit bowl
of coarse, pink glass, blossoming
with fruits and altar flame.
With its expressive cult gesture
and inward movement,
it acquires its genetic security,
freed from restraint and enthroned
like the eros of Socrates –
ugly,
but bursting with longing for beauty . . .

Old Man on the Bench

Life-flame flickers in his useless body.
Such magical yearning
beneath his prosaic misery you suddenly
see all the tools with which
he created his divinity of spirit,
                              surrounded by festivity.
As if at that very moment his existence had multiplied
in more valuable humans, societies and nations,
in millions of perfect worlds in the infinite,
where like an underlying principle
he finally imposed justice
and the beginnings of new life . . .

Apart from that, the old man does nothing. He rests,
gifting himself with a sublime expression.

On the Path

At the hour when the ready world
of the mountain turns philosophical
and dusk like drizzle speckles the light,
in the spaces pausing for thought,
'Good evening!' you hear.
'Good evening!'
you reply to the stranger
(no stranger
to himself) . . .

And you detect an ancient,
supreme liveliness in nature,
as if at that moment old stags
were arranging their statues and watching
for the geometry of the spirit . . .

In Athens Museum

I walked as in a jungle of objects,
indifferent towards the world of exhibits.
Their closed ranks put me off.
That was until I saw a heavy
green head of weathered bronze −
vivid, with a heartrending grimace,
straining on its metal base.
The inscription said it belonged to
an Olympic competitor . . . who was probably beaten,
with tousled curls, eyes and jawbone
wild from defeat. *Possibly Lysistratus*,
the inscription averred. However that may be,
his affliction is there for all to see.

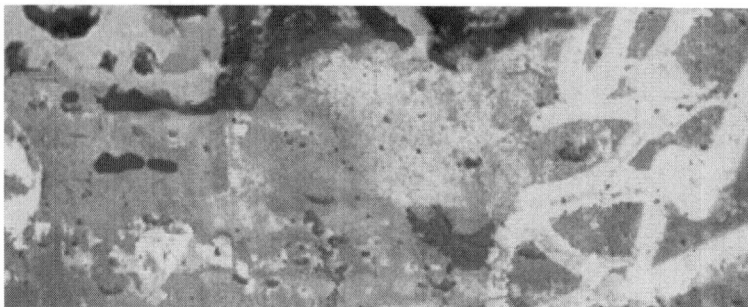

Louis Aragon
Lilac and Roses
Translated by Tom Chamberlain

Blossom time. Just what's in store, that, no one knows.
May without a cloud and June, knifed in the back.
I shall not forget the lilac and the rose
Nor other blooms that Spring kept folded in her pack.

I shall not forget the sadness, promises broken,
The procession, the shouting, the sun, the refugees,
The tanks the Belgians sent as their love-token,
The shuddering air, the road like the drone of bees.

All that bravado, spoiling for a fight;
(Wounds and kisses, both alike are red)
The lads up in their turrets, off to death's dark night,
Smothered with lilac by a people off its head.

I shall not forget the gardens, gold and green,
Of France, pages of missals from the olden days.
Those anxious evenings – what does the silence mean?
And roses, roses everywhere along the ways.

Panic flies on the wind, the flowers as calm as ever,
Mocking the soldiers riding on wings of fear.
The bicycles are crazy, the guns not really clever –
Unhappy campers with their pathetic gear.

I don't know why, but always I come back
– So many pictures swirling in my mind –
To Sainte Marthe, a general, the branches almost black,
A house in Normandy, the woods behind.

All quiet. Out in the dark, the enemy, you could say, dozes.
That was the night, they told us, Paris fell.
I shall not forget the lilac and the roses
Nor the double loss of what we loved so well.

Bunches of Flanders lilac, bouquets for the first days.
Death paints the cheeks of the gentle dark, as ladies do,
And roses sweeten the retreat along the ways,
Bright like a distant bonfire, those roses of Anjou.

(1940)

Louis Aragon
'Epilogue'
Translated by John Manson

In *Commitment in Modern French Literature* (London, 1967, p. 112) Max Adereth comments that in 'Epilogue' Louis Aragon '[...] introduces a new metre, a 20-syllable line, so as to give his imagination "the size of reality"'. The aim of the long line is maintained throughout the sixty lines, sometimes falling a little short, with caesurae, and rhyming abba.

In this monologue, first published in 1960 when he was sixty-three, Aragon sets out a grand framework within which to arrive at conclusions about the value of his own life and also to give injunctions to the generations who will succeed him. By this time his literary and political lives had been in the public domain for many years and he includes very generalised reflections about his own experience (coloured indirectly by the recent revelations of the history of Stalinism) and concludes on metaphorical notes of hope. 'Epilogue' was read at Aragon's funeral ceremony 28 December 1982 at the headquarters of the French Communist Party.

My feeling is that, given the length of line and the range of the poem, translation is best served here by a kind of prose poem which retains the capitals of the original, including four at the caesurae. There is no punctuation in the original.

Epilogue

I stand on the threshold of life and death eyes cast down
hands empty and the sea whose swell I hear is a sea that
never gives up her dead and my essence will be scattered
after me my shattered dreams sold by auction See already my
words wither like a leaf on my moist lip

I'll write these lines with wide open arms that my pulse may
be felt racing Live or die I'll exceed my throat and my voice
my breath and my song I'm the reaper drunk with reaping
who is seen to lay flat his life and his field all agasp about
the time he's losing who hones and rehones his scythe to a
jelly

I've chosen to give my lines this scale of crucifixion and let
luck fall at random no matter where on me the knife of the
caesura When all's said and done I've to set a limit to my
disproportion to make a cloak of my fictions to the cut of
reality

Life will have passed like a vast ruined castle that every wind
blows through The draughts bang the doors and still no
room is enclosed There sit poor weary strangers who knows
why some armed The grass has grown so thick in the moat
that the portcullis can no longer be lowered

In this house at any rate old or young we're not at home
No one knows for certain what brings him here perhaps
everything is only a dream Some are cold others hungry
most of the people have a gnawing secret From time to time
faceless kings pass We fall to our knees before them

When I was young they told me the victory of the angels
would come soon Ah how I believed in it how I believed
in it Now look I'm old Time for the young is a fuse always
pendent in their eyes and what is left for the old is too heavy
and too short that the wind may change for them

They question themselves on the essentials on what is still
worthwhile that they dedicate themselves to They see the
little they've done roaming through this monstrous gantry
they leave The shadow preferred to the substance o poor
people the future which is for no one little ones who play in
the street what limitless pity I have for you

I see everything you have before you misfortune blood
weariness You'll have learned nothing from our illusions
understood nothing of our mistakes We'll have been of no
use to you You'll have to pay the price in your turn I see your
shoulder sag I see the furrow of habit on your forehead

Sure sure you'll tell me that it's always like that but as their
right think of all those who put their living fingers their
hands of flesh in the works to change all that and think of
those who didn't even question their prison Have we the right
to despair the right to stop a moment

And a day may come when you'll have on you the mad sun
of victory Remember that we've also known that that others
climbed to tear down the flag of servitude from the Acropolis
and that they've been thrown they and their glory still
gasping into the common grave of history

Remember that the battle never ends and to have won isn't
next to nothing and that everything is called into question
again from the moment that man is responsible for man
We've seen great things done but there were frightful things
for it isn't always easy to know where good and evil lie

You'll pass where we passed a short time ago I read you like
an open book I hear this heart which beats in you like a heart
it seems beating in myself I know how you'll wear it out and
how this cause dies in you goes silent How autumn takes off
her make-up and the silence around a winter rose

I don't say that to demoralise We must look at nothingness
straight in the face to be able to overcome it The song isn't
less beautiful when it wanes We must be able to hear it
elsewhere rising again like the echo in the hills We're not
alone in the world to sing and the opera is the sum of the
songs

The opera we must be able to keep its part and know even
that a voice may go silent Always know that the underlying
choir takes up the interrupted phrase Since the singer has
done what he could to the limit of his song what does it
matter if on the way you're going to abandon me like a
hypothesis

I leave you in my turn like the dancer who rises one last time
Don't cast it up in his face if he already gives away the ghost
he bears within him I can no longer make you other presents
than those of this dull light Men of tomorrow blow on the
coals It is for you to say what I see

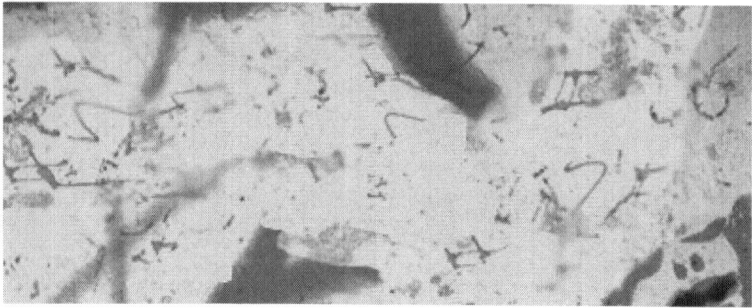

Homero Aridjis
Six Poems
Translated by George McWhirter

Homero Aridjis' poetry is best known in English through *Blue Spaces* (Seabury Press, 1974) and *Eyes to See Otherwise* (Carcanet and New Directions, 2002) in translations by Kenneth Rexroth, Eliot Weinberger, WS Merwin, Jerome Rothenberg and Betty Ferber. He was recently appointed Mexico's ambassador to UNESCO and is the President of *Grupo Cien* (100 artists for the environment) in Mexico.

The double

You went room to room
turning off the televisions
and the images of me sank
hollering into the nothing

At mirror after mirror
you covered your eyes
in order not see yourself
with my someone else's eyes.

Going through the hours
tearing up the photographs
while I looked on at you
from someone else's past.

Your silhouette standing
at the foot of a shared dream
cast two unfamiliar shadows
on the wall.

You did not recognize my name
nor I yours, you just kept looking at me
as strangely as the first time
we laid eyes on one another.

Recommendations for life as a ghost

When you go down the street, don't kiss the one you love.
Besides not seeing you, you might give her a fright.

When a car runs over you in the traffic,
don't fret, it will have flattened air.

In a room with a young naked girl, don't be upset
your desire will be a flutter in an empty jacket.

If, in the dawn, the cat is looking at you, don't stroke her,
her glowing eyes will be seeing nothing.

If your dog crosses through you without knowing you are
    there, don't be put out,
he will have seen a phantom calling to him from the other
    side of the light.

The mysterious Bermuda Triangle

The sea of solar silences
has swallowed up shiploads of words.

The sea of stellar unremembering
has swallowed myriad earthly images.

The sea of celestial vessels
has swallowed oceans of landscapes.

The sea of times without number
has swallowed the unbridled passions up.

The sea of irresistible forces,
the forever explained, inexplicable sea,

has swallowed itself up each night
without a trace or remorse.

Only you, creature of the moment, are immune
to the magnetic whirls and disappearances.

In a valley I saw the dead shades

In a valley I saw the shades of the dead
chasing beams of light in the morning.
Their feet trampling on dream's black apples
and hands passing through bodies and trees.
Busily the shades raced one after the other,
but as soon as convinced they had caught something,
the beams slid through their fingers
as if shades, hands, beams were nothing.

Black grass

Through the window I see your brother
out cutting the grass in the garden,
but he never finishes cutting
because when he has it cut over here
it has grown over there. It is black grass
sprouted from men's hearts
and it resembles grandfather's hair:
resistant to the scissors of wind.
Day and night I see your brother
out cutting death's grass for it.

Light pulsing on the rails

At dawn, pulses
of light run
along the rails,
their shadows
fallen along the sides.
At the speed of forgetting
they run toward
the ebony eye,
which also throbs.
Compare those pulses to your life.
Then, shut your eyes.

(All from *Solar Poems*, forthcoming from City Lights Publishers,
March 2010)

James Kirkup

James Kirkup died 10 May 2009 aged 91. Born in South Shields, the only son of a carpenter (see his luminous autobiography *The Only Child*), he read Modern Languages at Durham. During the war he was a conscientious objector and worked on farms. His first collection of poetry, *The Submerged Village and Other Poems*, was published by OUP in 1951. Thereafter he published a great deal, in many kinds of writing, and translated from several languages, notably French, German and Japanese. From the 1960s he lived much of his life abroad, chiefly in Japan and in Andorra, where he died.

Kirkup was a frequent and important contributor to *MPT*. He appeared first in Issue 9, January 1971, introducing the poetry of Takagi Kyozo and (with Nakano Michio) translating more than thirty of his poems. After that he is to be found in *MPT* 2/5, 6 and 8, with translations of German, French and medieval Arabo-Andalusian poems, and an article on haiku. But the best place to get to know him as a translator is *MPT* 2/11, summer 1997, in a long and very considered appreciation by Daniel Weissbort with much quotation from his work and commentary on it.

Kirkup's poem 'The Love that Dares to Speak its Name', sex fantasy of the centurion left with Christ's dead body, published in *Gay News* in 1976, caused that newspaper to be successfully prosecuted for blasphemous libel. We thought of this *cause célèbre* three years ago, when we were putting together our 'Transgressions' issue, and phoned James Kirkup in Andorra to ask if he'd like to contribute any reflections on his poem and the fuss. Quite rightly, he declined. It was all done with, long ago. We mention it now, in this 'Freed Speech' issue, because the common law offences of blasphemy and blasphemous libel have still not been abolished. On 11 July 2002, to commemorate the twenty-fifth anniversary of the *Gay News* case, Peter Tatchell and ten others read out a stanza each of the offending poem and invited prosecution. The police filmed the proceedings and sent this evidence to the DPP, who decided not to bother. We wrote to the British Humanist Association to ask what they thought would happen if we published the poem. They couldn't be sure, but said they'd be delighted if we'd try it out. Hm, we thought. With two or three clicks you can get your very own copy of 'The Love that Dares to Speak its Name' off the web. Whatever its virtues, they are not poetic. Hardly seemed worth the risk for a publication we should not be able to defend on poetic grounds.

As in the case of Michael Hamburger, we had dealings with James Kirkup on the threshold and across the threshold of death. Last year he sent us some *tanka* versions of Rimbaud, which we accepted and wrote to him, asking for the usual brief note. We never heard back. We shall print them in the next issue, 'Transplants'.

David and Helen Constantine

Reviews

Stéphane Mallarmé
Sonnets
Translated by David Scott
Shearsman Books
ISBN978-1905700-42-4
126 pp £9.95

Accepting French Symbolism as central to the development of European Modernism and Mallarmé's specific role as a key innovator of notions of the *signe*, the space of the page, and the poem's three-dimensional potential, one is initially wary of what one will find in attempts to realise the impossible act of translating his verse. Yet one is often pleasantly surprised at the comprehensibility of the resulting translations. That said, it is the brave translator that embarks on such a task.

David Scott in his bi-lingual text has opted for Mallarmé's sonnets rather than a 'greatest hits' and the resulting Shearsman volume (appropriately marketed towards undergraduates) with its erudite twenty-six page introduction builds on the ideas of Clive Scott who has written widely on French Modernism (see *MPT* 3/6 for my review of his *Translating Rimbaud's Illuminations*, University of Exeter Press). This is a debt readily acknowledged by David Scott in his dedication to Scott – à la Dante to Arnaut Daniel – as *il miglior fabbro* (the better craftsman). Clive Scott's work always provides challenging and stimulating reading and David Scott offers us comparable complexity in his introduction though occasionally requiring us to do a double take – not a text to be embarked on after a late night.

He begins by outlining key stages in Mallarmé's development emphasising his huge impact on poetic theory, given that he was essentially an 'occasional poet' who had to balance his writing with the gruelling job of school teacher for which he was ill-equipped. For Scott the thirty-nine sonnets presented here epitomise Mallarmé's key concerns in that they reflect 'a radical point of both continuity and discontinuity within a long tradition of European poetic expression and at the same time embody a uniquely modern synthesis of language's multiple potentialities'.

Scott goes on to provide us with some close analysis of specific sonnets and Mallarmé's treatment of individual words. He draws on the theories of both Jean-Pierre Richard and Jacques Derrida to illustrate the impossibility of translating the whole range of Mallarmé's effects, yet at the same time he rather conveniently lets the translator off the hook allowing him or her to act as a fellow traveller in attempting to equate language with a total account of experience – the key lies in not regarding the translation as something completed or closed but rather:

> language, verse, poetry, theory, signification, translation – all are part of an ongoing system or series of interrelated systems in which the pleasure and satisfaction of engagement would be as rewarding as the arrival at any – necessarily provisional – point of completion.

But what of the translations themselves? After a few questionable choices in the early poems such as in 'Futile Request' where 'comme je ne suis pas ton bichon embarbé' is translated as 'As I am not your toy-boy or designer-stubbled mate' – a line that is inappropriately modern – these sonnets stand up extremely well. Scott is particularly good at achieving both a fierce fidelity to stanza form and rhyme combined with sharp cohesion and the

use of strong active verbs. Take his superb version of the second
poem of 'Plusieurs Sonnets II':

> Can the pure and lovely and lively new day
> Tear open with a stroke of its ecstatic wing
> The hidden lake beneath the ice slumbering
> Haunted by glaciers of flights that did not stray!
>
> A swan from the past, remembering, can portray
> Itself grandly circling in a despairing ring
> Above the region it was unable to sing
> When of sterile winter set in the bright dismay.
>
> Its long neck will shake off the white agony
> Space inflicts on the bird that denies it any,
> But not the icy ground where its plumage is caught.
>
> Phantom assigning to this place its pure icon,
> It is stilled by a contemptuous daydream that sought
> To clothe in cold exile uselessly the Swan.

Mallarmé's extended metaphor of the swan to represent the
new day is itself wonderful and there is a frighteningly cold
impression of the futility of the swan's attempt to surface through
the winter's cold. The poem describes a non-event established by
the question at the start so that we are getting what the swan does
not manage to do, leaving us with a bleak view of both experience
and the natural world. Scott has more than done the poem justice.
Space doesn't allow much direct comparison with the original
but it is striking, *faux amis* apart, how often he keeps close to
the diction of the original. In general one might consider this a
dangerous strategy leading to poetry that reads as translation,
but Scott seems to have got it just right giving the impression
that if something works don't change it. The strong lines 'Its
long neck will shake off the white agony / Space inflicts on the
bird that denies it any' for example is near enough word-for-word

Mallarmé. Another strength is the way he manages to be faithful
to the rhyme scheme at the same time as he overlays the poem
with run-on lines that prevent the rhyme sounding forced or too
regular. This gives the poem a powerful cadence and allows the
metaphor to travel comfortably through the poem suggesting the
swan's movements. It is this technical skill and poetic feel which
allows him to interweave fidelity and creativity fairly consistently
throughout the collection thus offering a sound bi-lingual text
for all students of Mallarmé – further supplemented by very
detailed supporting notes and a good selective bibliography. All
in all a remarkable achievement.

Belinda Cooke

Katerina Anghelaki-Rooke
The Scattered Papers of Penelope: New and Selected Poems
Edited by Karen Van Dyck
Anvil Press Poetry
128pp, paperback, £9.95
ISBN: 978-0-85646-401-0

Godchild of none other than Nikos Kazantzakis, already an
established poet in her early twenties and producing fourteen
collections over the course of four decades, which saw her win
most major poetry prizes in Greece, Katerina Anghelaki-Rooke
has also been fortunate when it comes to translation. As Karen
Van Dyck explains at one point in her engaging and thoroughly
researched Introduction, some of the best translators of Greek
poetry – among them, Kimon Friar and Rae Dalven – have been
involved with her work, even though many of these translations
have until now indeed been scattered, existing in old literary
journals and small press publications. The poet is also fortunate
to have Van Dyck, a Modern Greek Literature Professor at
Columbia, sift through and select, with her help, the best
translations (in many cases, assisted *self-translations*) of her poems.

The resulting volume, including new renderings by Van Dyck, is published by Anvil, home to Greek poets of the calibre of Seferis, Elytis and Gatsos.

The title here, borrowed from that of an early collection, also serves as a first marker of Anghelaki-Rooke's thematic preoccupations. In their monologues and narratives, her Penelopes and Helens relate the female side of myth, truths of women's experience in an urgent present tense:

And Penelope who now hears
the evocative music of fear
the cymbals of resignation
the sweet song of a quiet day
without sudden changes of weather and tone
the complex chords
of an infinite gratitude
for what did not happen, was not said, cannot be uttered
now signals no, no, no more loving
no more words and whispers
caresses and bites
small cries in the darkness
scent of flesh that burns in the light.
Pain was the most exquisite suitor
and she slammed the door on him.

('The Other Penelope', trans. Edmund and Mary Keeley)

Anghelaki-Rooke is a superb anatomist of psychologies of passion: her stories of all-consuming desire trace every shade of feeling, the poet's conversational style assembling the minutes of consciousness and memory, either in prose poems or in a fluid free verse where stanza breaks are often unnecessary. Her language is always direct and accessible, yet tinged with sadness and populated by contemplated wounds, pausing for potent images that often perfectly capture alternating moods or stirrings of the mind. In 'The Red Moon' the poet sees 'blond women smile and

disappear under the broken/ plaster' of her house, while the dog
'with his stomach heavy from all the tenderness / of my barren
heart, empties his guts on the black earth'. Various cultural
and religious signifiers – cicadas, angels, monks – also feature;
but together with everyday objects and anchors of the Greek
landscape, they serve mostly as points of entry and return to the
poet's interiors – or those of inhabited, surrogate selves.

Though this poetry can seem intensely personal and
autobiographical, it is too interested in the world, in meaning-
making, in the consequences of choices made, to merit the
negative connotations of 'confessional'. Rather, its significance
lies in how it consistently finds the natural world and inner
life, soul and body in peculiar unison or interdependence. In
Anghelaki-Rooke's art, it is indeed the body, with its manifold
needs and sensations, wounds and imperatives that, as Van Dyck
and others before her have observed, negotiates thought, memory,
and ultimately, acts of writing.

If poetry, poems and language increasingly become central
characters, parts of the examined life, or inform imagery and
metaphors, it is translation which most poignantly allows passion
and literature to define each other:

Because I cannot touch you
with my tongue
I transliterate my passion.
[...]
Because I cannot undress you
I imagine you in the clothes
of a foreign language.
Because I cannot nestle
under your wing
I fly around you
turning the pages of your dictionary.
I want to learn how you bare yourself

how you open yourself up.
That's why I search
between the lines
[...]

      ('Translating Life's End into Love', trans. Karen Van Dyck)

It is perhaps not surprising for a poet who has produced exquisite Greek versions of, among others, Seamus Heaney, Dylan Thomas and Joseph Brodsky (as well as English renderings of her own work) and who once stated that 'poetry is a free translation of reality', to articulate translation as part of literary endeavour, and as a potent metaphor for desire and possession.

   Despite such self-observation, and even though Anghelaki-Rooke's work carries its fair share of linguistic play and intertextual allusion (together with the layers of a tongue evolving relatively uninterrupted for millennia), it avoids the dead ends of language-oriented experiment. Her keen exploration of what one of her sequences names 'The Narrative of the Self' rarely deflects the lyricism and immediacy of her expression, the poet always seeking to phrase living tissue, make every emotion tactile. It is what allows her voice to retain so much of its vitality and clarity in English, and through the prism of the many capable hands at work here, including her own.

Paschalis Nikolaou

Paths of the Beggar Woman. The Selected Poems
of Marina Tsvetaeva
Translated by Belinda Cooke
Tonbridge, Kent: Worple Press, 2008
ISBN 978-1-905208-11-1
143 pp. £12

Tsvetaeva's poetry presents many challenges to the translator. It is true in her case more than most that no single translation will ever do justice to the original. This should not deter us from trying to translate her, however: the more translations we have, the closer those who do not know Russian can come to an appreciation of her work. This new volume of selected poems of Marina Tsvetaeva is a welcome addition to the existing corpus of translations. It offers a generous selection of poems from across Tsvetaeva's career and, in particular, many from the early, pre-revolutionary period. It is also valuable that cycles of poems are presented in their entirety: the poems to Aleksandr Blok and to Akhmatova are part of the rich and important dialogue between Russian poets of the Silver Age, and are most meaningful when kept together as they were organised by Tsvetaeva herself. The notes provided give useful information to those unacquainted with this background, and may be a helpful steer for anyone wishing to read more Russian poetry of the period.

Belinda Cooke makes judicious choices in her approach to the task. She sensibly abandons any idea of reproducing the end rhymes of the original, seeking instead to introduce internal rhyme where possible, and so preserve a sense of harmony. Her handling of rhythms is similarly careful, although one cannot help but lament the loss of some of the more staccato, striking and effective lines in which Russian monosyllables predominate. The final stanza of 'Longing for Home', for example, loses its heightened intensity when the rhythm and rhymes of the original are abandoned. A similar evening out of the tone is created in poems where some of Tsvetaeva's exclamation marks and dashes have been omitted. The question of what to do with so many exclamations confronts all her translators, and most agree that some have to be left out in English versions, but in places their omission changes the tone. 'Yesterday he still looked me in the eyes,/ but now he just turns to one side' suggests a dejected and subdued tone without the concluding exclamation mark found in the Russian. More seriously, in 'A Dialogue Between Hamlet and his Conscience' the speech markers have been omitted, rendering the two parts of the dialogue indistinguishable.

The chief tone of the collection is lyrical and somewhat subdued, and this is partly due to the choice of poems: the cycle 'Insomnia', for example, is softer than many of the well-known poems which reach all the high notes. This tone seems also to have been informed by Cooke's reading of Tsvetaeva's work and life. Her title and introduction draw attention to the tragedy of her experiences from 1917 until her suicide in 1941, which is essential background knowledge for readers of the poems written during these years. It is worth remembering, however, that more than half of the poems in this collection date from before 1917, when Tsvetaeva still belonged to the privileged classes in Russia. It is not that in these poems she does not fashion herself as the heroine of tragedy: she does. But the essentially literary nature of this pose is very different from her later despair, and the knowing, self-conscious construction of her literary self does not always come through in Cooke's translations of the early poems; some of their playfulness is simply lost. In several places, the sense of a line is changed through slips such as a change in the positioning of negation. Cooke's 'I am glad, that you are not sick because of me' has lost the nuance of the original 'I am glad your lovesickness is not over me' and, in the same poem, 'I am glad . . . you do not want me to burn in hell . . . because I do not kiss you' is far chaster than Tsvetaeva's 'I am glad...you do not want me to burn in hell . . . because it is not you I'm kissing'.

The lyrical tone of these translations suits most of the poems, however, and the collection often conveys Tsvetaeva's voice most effectively. Though occasionally Cooke observes a loyalty to the Russian that results in literalness, there are many bold and successful renderings: the canonical 'An Attempt at Jealousy' is wonderfully translated here, as is 'Phaedra', 'Ophelia to Hamlet', and 'Ophelia in Defence of the Queen'. The poems to Akhmatova are particularly polished, capturing the frequent shifts in register that juxtapose awed respect with the tone of an everyday, affectionate exchange. This collection is valuable for its steady faithfulness to the original, its breadth of poems, and in particular for the inclusion of so many of the pre-revolutionary poems.

Emily Lygo

Further Books: Writing Women

Almond, Maureen, *Chasing the Ivy*, Biscuit Publishing, paperback, 66 pages, ISBN: 978-1-903914-37-3, £7.99

Jansma, Esther, *What It Is: Selected Poems*, translated by Francis R Jones, Bloodaxe Books, paperback. 96pp, ISBN: 978-1-85224-780-5, £8.95

Eden,Vivian, *Front and Back*, Carmel Publishers, paperback, 144pp, ISBN: 978-965-407-910-5

Merini, Alda, *Love Lessons: Selected Poems of Alda Merini*, translated by Susan Stewart, Princeton University Press, hardback, 144pp, ISBN: 978-0-691-12938-9, £11.95

Manner, Eeva-Liisa, *Bright, Dusky, Bright*. translated by Emily Jeremiah, Waterloo Press, paperback, 112 pp, ISBN: 978-1-906742-15-7, £9

Verdaguer, Jacint, *Selected Poems of Jacint Verdaguer* (bilingual edition), edited and translated by Ronald Puppo, University of Chicago Press, hardback, 340pp, ISBN: 978-0-226-8530-0, £20

The worlds of satire, academia, political and religious divides and erotic passion are not always viewed as the preserve of women poets, more likely, it is often assumed, to concern themselves with domesticity or romantic love. The poets and translators included in this edition's round up, however, prove such prejudices wrong in style, pushing such traditional boundaries with great skill and vigour.

Maureen Almond's original and engaging *Chasing the Ivy* is a case in point, reworking the often difficult and therefore sometimes neglected satire of Latin poet Horace's *Odes* in the context of the contemporary literary scene. As its titles reveal – 'Ode to An Arvon Course Writer', 'Ode to Naïve Poets', or 'Ode to the Poetry Professor at the End of Term', this proves a rich source of satirical material, offering the reader not only a wry smile at the foibles of contemporary poetry but a new point of access to the Roman poet's intricate web of reference. As in Almond's previous volume *The Works*, also based on Horace's often vituperative poetry, the juxtaposition between ancient and modern proves both entertaining and enlightening, showcasing Almond's deft wit and sure phrasing, a fine match for its original source. As 'Ode to the Editor' concludes: 'My *mind* is all *I* open, by the way. /You need to know that *my* words aren't just verbals./As for me I'm not prepared to lie/to earn my laurels.' With *Chasing the Ivy*, Almond can safely rest on hers.

Dutch poet Esther Jansma is also concerned with the effect of the classical past on the present, inspired by her other job as an archaeologist and dendrochronologist for Dutch Heritage. Francis R Jones' typically crafted translations provide the first full length volume available in English, including the fascinating poems she wrote on Hadrian's Wall in 2004 as part of an Arts UK project which included writers from all the countries that originally garrisoned Hadrian's Wall. Jansma's revelatory poetry explores the layers we all excavate, from the personal – the stillbirth of a child, the loss of a parent – to the universal. As 'Archaeology 1' explains, her highly individual voice is that of 'the rag-and-bone man, collector/of odds and ends, moments,/cracks in things, braille/is forever decoding expressions/of the selfsame face.'

American-Israeli poet Vivian Eden also engages with the deep-rooted concerns of the past and the ways in which they still reverberate through the troubled present; 'Within the core,' as 'Time's Arrow, Time's Cycle' notes, 'the poems churn/The silt of days spread fine'. An assured first collection, *Front and Back*, represents a bilingual project with Hebrew translations from various poets and translators bound in the back of her English volume. Eden's graceful lyrics revisit her American homeland as well as reach down to the very core of her adopted city Jerusalem, revealing a great strength and depth in their delicacy. She has noted how, on being asked at a reading to eschew political poems, 'all the poems were immediately political'. As the conclusion of 'Solving the Problem' witnesses: 'Only two stars will punctuate/ the cypresses outside the window./You will say: "Were it darker/ we would see more."'

Dream-like figures from a mythic and poetic past also stalk Alda Merini's intense poetry – Cleopatra, Orpheus, the Cumaean Sibyl – as well as more recent role models such as Emily Dickinson or Sylvia Plath. One of Italy's most important and beloved living poets, Merini began her long career as a Modernist in the 1950s but later spent twenty years in mental hospitals, re-emerging in the 1970s with a renewed vigour for her work. Her vibrant verse is here extremely well-served by noted American poet Susan Stewart's translations, capturing the essence of Merini's dark and passionate poetry where 'The most superb thing is the night/ when the last threats tumble/and the soul throws itself into adventure'.

By contrast, acclaimed Finnish poet Eeva-Liisa Manner's work is subtle and ethereal, mysterious, but equally compelling. In Emily Jeremiah's dexterous translations – awarded a 2008 Stephen Spender Prize as well as previously featured in *MPT* 3/9 – Manner's stark landscapes shimmer again with mesmerising poetic vision:. 'let's tread lightly/though strange times,' suggests 'Sub rosa', 'shifting twilight,/the soughing, remembering forest of autumn days/not scolding sorrow. It is ours, and still warm'. This is a revelatory volume which cannot be recommended highly enough.

Finally, the nineteenth-century Catalan poet Jacint Verdaguer might have a Y chromosome but his epic verse, if rather more florid than Manner's, is equally visionary and mystical. Ronald Puppo's major new edition should help to ensure the wide new readership it deserves, offering faithful and highly readable versions of Verdaguer's epic and religious verse made even more accessible by helpful notes and introductory comments. As Puppo's version of 'The Harp' concludes: 'there in the flowering of the stars, born amid/shadowing wings of the lovely evening,/ smiling at me, divine aurora,/I saw the Catalan Muse in the heavens.' Here, as Puppo promises in his excellent introduction, 'English readers might catch a glimpse of many Verdaguerian rainbows.'

I would like to end by noting that this will be my final round-up as Reviews Editor for *MPT*. Over the last five years it has been a fascinating and richly rewarding task to discover so many new poets – or indeed known poets and works reinvented through new translations and versions – as well as to see at first hand how vital and essential the publishing of poetry in translation remains in Britain. I will miss the many wonderful books that have arrived on my doorstep but wish all their creators, translators, publishers, not to forget their readers, every future success and pleasure in keeping such truly high quality alive and well.

Josephine Balmer

Our new Reviews Editor is Saradha Soobrayen

Books for review should be sent to The Editors, *Modern Poetry in Translation*, Queen's College, Oxford, OX1 4AW.

An Apology, Thanks and Acknowledgements

Notes on Nasrin Parvaz and Hubert Moore got left out of the last issue's 'Notes on Contributors'. We apologize, and include them among the contributors to this issue.

Thanks to Dave Horrocks and Martina Lauster for their help with Heine and the censors.

We are grateful to the following for permissions:

Suhrkamp, the Brecht Estate and A & C Black, for the translations of Brecht
Suhrkamp for the translations of Kaschnitz
Jean Ristat for the translation of Aragon's 'Epilogue'
Heaventree Press for the poems from *See How I Land*.

Amit Chaudhuri's poem 'The Writers' first appeared in the *Observer*.

Notes on Contributors

Annemarie Austin was born in Devon and grew up on the Somerset Levels and in Weston-super-Mare, where she has lived for most of her life. She is the author of six collections of poetry, the most recent of which is *Very: New and Selected Poems* (Bloodaxe 2008).

Josephine Balmer's books include *Sappho: Poems and Fragments*; *Classical Women Poets*; *Catullus: Poems of Love and Hate* and *Chasing Catullus: Poems, Translations and Transgressions* (all Bloodaxe). Her latest volume, *The Word for Sorrow* (much of which first appeared in *MPT*) was published by Salt earlier this year.

Chris Beckett grew up in Ethiopia in the 1960s. He won the *Poetry London* competition in 2001 and his first collection, *The Dog Who Thinks He's a Fish*, was published in 2004. He is working on a collection of praise poems about boyhood in Ethiopia.

Tom Boll was the Assistant Director of the Poetry Translation Centre from 2004-2007. He has written on Latin American poetry and co-translated the Mexican poet Coral Bracho with Katherine Pierpoint (Enitharmon Press, 2008). His first book, *Octavio Paz and T. S. Eliot: Modern Poetry and the Translation of Influence*, will be published by Legenda in 2010. He teaches in the department of Spanish and Spanish American Studies at King's College London.

Tom Chamberlain, son of a dock worker, enjoyed his Grammar School at Cleethorpes, graduated in Social Science at Nottingham. He taught art for twenty-five years in secondary schools and in retirement leads groups for the University of the Third Age in philosophy, Latin and drawing. His wife died in 1999, leaving two children, a daughter living in France, with two French grandchildren.

Amit Chaudhuri is one of the leading novelists of his generation. His latest book is *The Immortals*, his fifth novel. He is also an acclaimed essayist and musician. Among the prizes he has won are the Commonwealth Writers Prize, the Encore Award, the *Los Angeles Times* Book Prize, and the Sahitya Akademi award. He is Professor of Contemporary Literature at the University of East Anglia, and a Fellow of the Royal Society of Literature.

Tom Cheesman is Senior Lecturer in German at Swansea University, and runs Hafan Books (www.hafan.org). Translator with John Goodby of Soleïman Adel Guémar's *State of Emergency* (Arc Visible Poets, 2007).

David Constantine's most recent translation is of Goethe's *Faust II*.

Peter Constantine's most recent translations are Sophocles' *Three Theban Plays* (Barnes & Noble Classics, 2008) and *The Essential Writings of Machiavelli* (Modern Library, 2007). He was awarded the PEN Translation Prize for *Six Early Stories*, by Thomas Mann, and the National Translation Award for *The Undiscovered Chekhov*.

Belinda Cooke has published one collection of poetry, *Resting Place* (Flarestack 2007), and a collection of translations, *Paths of the Beggarwoman: the Selected Poems of Marina Tsvetaeva* (Worple Press 2008). Boris Poplavsky's *Flags*, produced in collaboration with Richard McKane, is forthcoming with Shearsman Press (2009) and she is currently working with Richard McKane on Boris Pasternak's *Zhivago Poems and Other Later Poems*.

Dawood was born in Afghanistan in 1989, and came to the UK in 2006.

Jonathan Dunne's translations have been nominated for the Independent Foreign Fiction Prize and the Warwick Prize for Writing, among others. In 2010, Harvill Secker publishes his translation of *Books Burn Badly* by Manuel Rivas and Shearsman Books his translation of *The Seventh Gesture* by Tsvetanka Elenkova (authors who appeared in *MPT* 3/7 and 3/8 respectively).

Julian Farmer is a forty-eight-year-old poet and translator of five or six languages who lives in Guildford, works in a shop and cooks for his family. He has recently studied Classical Languages, French and Russian and has had poems and translations published in *The London Magazine*, *Acumen*, *The Shop*, *Agenda* and *Stand*.

Jennie Feldman's first collection, *The Lost Notebook* (Anvil, 2005) was shortlisted for the Glen Dimplex Poetry Award. Her translations of the French poet Jacques Réda, *Treading Lightly: Selected Poems 1961–1975*, were also published by Anvil in 2005. She is co-translator and editor, with Stephen Romer, of *Into the Deep Street: Seven Modern French Poets (1938–2008)*, a bilingual anthology published by Anvil in June 2009. She lives in Jerusalem.

Michael Foley has published four novels, four collections of poetry (most recently *Autumn Beguiles the Fatalist*) and a collection of free translations from French poets. His first non-fiction prose book, *The Age of Absurdity*, will appear in February 2010 and A *New and Selected Poems* will follow.

John Greening (born 1954) received a Cholmondeley Award in 2008. His *Hunts: Poems 1979–2009*, containing highlights from eleven earlier collections, was recently published by Greenwich Exchange for whom he has produced studies of the First World War Poets, Yeats, Edward Thomas, Hardy and Ted Hughes.

Harry Guest collaborated with Goshi Masayo over her translations of Stevie Smith into Japanese which appeared in

Tokyo last year. His *Comparisons & Conversions* containing his most recent translations came out from Shearsman this January.

Seamus Heaney was awarded the Nobel Prize in 1995. His most recent book of poems is *District and Circle* (2006). *Stepping Stones: Interviews with Seamus Heaney* by Dennis O'Driscoll came out last year.

William Heath was born in London in 1980 and is a graduate of Bretton Hall College. He is self-taught in the Ancient Greek language and over the last few years has been working on the fragments of Archilochos, Sappho, Alkaios, Ibykos and Anakreon. This is his first published translation.

Mike Horwood was born in London in 1955 and now lives in Finland. He has recently completed an online MA in Creative Writing at Manchester Metropolitan University. His translation from the Finnish of Martti Hynynen's collection, *island, nameless rock*, is published by Cinnamon Press.

Robert Hull's books of poetry are: *Encouraging Shakespeare, Stargrazer, Everest and Chips* and *On Portsmouth Station* (Beafred, 2008). His titles for children include history, poetry anthologies, and retellings of myth. He has written two books about teaching: *Behind the Poem* (Routledge 1988), a scrutiny and celebration of children's writing; and *The Language Gap* (Methuen), a critical account of language practices in schooling.

Sarah Kafatou is a painter and writer living in London.

Steve Komarnyckyj is a British Ukrainian writer and linguist whose literary translations and poems have appeared in *Poetry Salzburg Review, Vsesvit, The North* and the *Echo Room*. See also www.holodomor.org.uk

Emily Lygo studied Russian at the University of Oxford, where she completed her D. Phil in 2006. She is now Lecturer in Russian at the University of Exeter. Her main research interest is Russian poetry, and she has translated the work of Tatiana Voltskaia (Bloodaxe, 2006).

John Manson is a critic, translator and poet. He has co-edited two selections of Hugh MacDiarmid's poetry and published over fifty articles on Scottish and European authors. In 1995 he was awarded the Scottish Arts Council's first bursary for translation.

Jamie McKendrick, born in Liverpool in 1955, has published five books of poems and a book of selected poems, *Sky Nails*. His most recent book is *Crocodiles & Obelisks* (Faber, 2007). He has also translated Giorgio Bassani's novel, *The Garden of the Finzi-Continis* (Penguin Modern Classics, 2007) and is the editor of *The Faber Book of 20th-Century Italian Poems*. His translation of the poems of Valerio Magrelli will be published in 2010.

George McWhirter has just completed his term as Vancouver's first Poet Laureate (2007-2009). His most recent book of verse is *The Anachronicles* (Ronsdale Press, 2008) and his Vancouver Poet Laureate project, *A Verse Map of Vancouver* (Anvil Press, 2009) explores the city through poems by eighty-seven poets and photographs by Derek von Essen.

F.Mehrban is a pseudonym. 'Mehrban' is a word that means 'kind' in Farsi. If the author's real name were to be used on publication, family members remaining in Iran might be in danger.

Hubert Moore's latest collection is *The Hearing Room* (Shoestring, 2006).

John Morey is an English graduate living in Portsmouth. His interest in translation started with Homer and now he is working on Dante's *Commedia*. He writes, 'Taking *Purgatorio* as a starting point, canto by canto I alter and subvert it, so by the latter cantos it becomes a new poem.'

Paschalis Nikolaou received his Ph.D. from the University of East Anglia, and is currently a teaching and research fellow at the Ionian University (Corfu). Reviews, essays, translations and poems have appeared in English and Greek literary magazines and research journals. He has co-edited *Translating Selves: Experience and Identity Between Languages and Literatures* (Continuum, 2008).

Bernard O'Donoghue is a leading Irish poet, critic and medieval scholar. He was born in Cork in 1945 and moved to England in 1962. Since 1965 he has lived in Oxford, where he teaches English at Wadham College. His *Selected Poems* was published by Faber in 2008.

Nasrin Parvaz's activities in human and civil rights in Tehran led to her imprisonment in Evin Prison from 1982 to 1990. Her book about her prison experience, *Beneath the Narcissus*, has been published in Farsi and Italian.

Yousif Qasmiyeh was a teacher at schools run by the United Nations Relief and Works Agency in Palestinian refugee camps across Lebanon before coming to the UK in 2004. He completed his undergraduate and postgraduate studies in English Language and Literature at the Lebanese University, where he also participated in a number of poetry festivals. He has published his poetry in *An-Nahar*, and is working on his first collection of poetry. He is also translating a selection of poems by Jamie McKendrick into Arabic.

Shazea Quraishi was born in Pakistan, emigrated to Canada aged ten, and lived in Madrid before moving to London where she works as a writer and translator. Her poems have been published in anthologies and magazines in the UK and the US.

Padraig Rooney was born in Ireland in 1956. *In The Bonsai Garden* (Raven Arts Press) won the Patrick Kavanagh Award for poetry in 1986. His second collection *The Escape Artist* (Smith/ Doorstop) won The Poetry Business competition in 2006. He has received two bursaries from the Irish Arts Council and is the 2009 winner of the Strokestown International Poetry Prize. He lives in Basel, Switzerland.

Carole Satyamurti's most recent collection of poetry is *Stitching the Dark: New and Selected Poems* (Bloodaxe, 2005). She is currently working on a verse retelling of the *Mahabharata*.

Sudeep Sen was awarded a Hawthornden Fellowship (UK) and nominated for a Pushcart Prize (USA) for poems included in *Postmarked India: New & Selected Poems* (Harper Collins). More recently, he has published *Prayer Flag, Distracted Geographies, Rain,* and *Aria* (translations). His poetry has been translated into twenty-five languages. He is the editor of *Atlas,* and lives in New Delhi.

Helen Smith is a novelist and playwright, the author of two cult novels, *Alison Wonderland* and *Being Light*, two children's books, and several plays and screenplays, many of which feature original poetry as part of the text.

Adam J. Sorkin recently published *Memory Glyphs*, a collection of three Romanian prose poets, Cristian Popescu, Iustin Panţa and Radu Andriescu (Twisted Spoon, 2009) and Ruxandra Cesereanu's *Crusader-Woman*, translated with Cesereanu (Black Widow, 2008). Distinguished Professor of English, Penn State Brandywine, Sorkin is the most active translator of Romanian poetry in the English-speaking world.

Elżbieta Wójcik-Leese has published English versions of contemporary Polish poetry in the UK, Ireland, USA and Nepal. *Salt Monody* is her selection from Marzanna Kielar (see *MPT* 3/2). A volume by Krystyna Miłobędzka is forthcoming from Arc in 2010. She is a contributing editor to *Poetry Wales* and co-edits *Przekładaniec*. She lives in Copenhagen.

THE BIG GREEN ISSUE

Edited by David and Helen Constantine

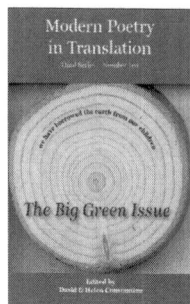

Cover by Lucy Wilkinson

Contents

Rose Scooler, 'Mica Parade', translated by Sibyl Ruth
Tomas Venclova, three poems, translated by Ellen Hinsey
Peace, Poetry and Palestine
Franz Hodjak, six poems, translated by Peter Oram
Zsuzsa Beney, five poems, translated by George Szirtes
Cesare Pavese, five poems, translated by David Douglas
Eugeniusz Tkaczyszyn-Dycki, five poems, translated by Bill
Johnston
Jerzy Harasymowicz, four poems, translated by Maria
Rewakowicz, with illustrations by Swava Harasymowicz
Eugene Dubnov, two poems, translated, with the author, by
Vernon Scannell, Anne Ridler and John Heath-Stubbs

Reviews
Cecilia Rossi, on translations of Pura López-Colomé, Dulce María
Loynaz and Mercedes Roffé
Paschalis Nikolaou on Richard Burns's *The Blue Butterfly*
Belinda Cooke on Sasha Dugdale's Elena Shvarts
David Constantine on *Poems from Guantánamo* and two Hafan Books
Josephine Balmer, Further Reviews

Price £9.95
    Available from www.mptmagazine.com

FRONTIERS

Edited by David and Helen Constantine

Cover by Lucy Wilkinson

Contents

J.S. Tennant, 'The Sleeper in the Valley' (after Rimbaud)
Brecht, ten poems, translated by David Constantine

Reviews
Belinda Cooke, on translations of Jean Cassou and Aldo Vianello
Charlie Louth, on the Bachmann-Celan correspondence
Josephine Balmer, Further Reviews

Price £9.95
Available from www.mptmagazine.com

MPT Subscription Form

Name	Address
Phone	Postcode
E-mail	Country

I would like to subscribe to *Modern Poetry in Translation* (please tick relevant box):

Subscription Rates (including postage by surface mail)

	UK	Overseas
❏ One year subscription (2 issues)	£19.90	£25 / US$ 42
❏ Two year subscription (4 issues) with discount	£36	£46 / US$ 77

Student Discount*

	UK	Overseas
❏ One year subscription (2 issues)	£16	£21 / US$ 35
❏ Two year subscription (4 issues)	£28	£38 / US$ 63

Please indicate which year you expect to complete your studies 20 . . .

Standing Order Discount (only available to UK subscribers)

❏ Annual subscription (2 issues)	£18
❏ Student rate for annual subscription (2 issues)*	£14

Payment Method (please tick appropriate box)

❏ **Cheque:** please make cheques payable to: *Modern Poetry in Translation.*
Sterling, US Dollar and Euro cheques accepted.

❏ **Standing Order:** please complete the standing order request below, indicating the date you would like your first payment to be taken. This should be at least one month after you return this form. We will set this up directly with your bank. Subsequent annual payments will be taken on the same date each year. For UK only.

Bank Name	Account Name
Branch Address	❏ Please notify my bank
	Please take my first payment on
Post Code	......./......./......... and future payments on
Sort Code	the same date each year.
Account Number	Signature:
	Date........./........./............

Bank Use Only: In favour of Modern Poetry in Translation, Lloyds TSB, 1 High St, Carfax, Oxford, OX1 4AA, UK a/c 03115155 Sort-code 30-96-35

Please return this form to: The Administrator, Modern Poetry in Translation, The Queen's College, Oxford, OX1 4AW   administrator@mptmagazine/www.mptmagazine.com